"The way Kraig Kann helped us think about our "why" and helped us learn to dynamically present the Concero story has elevated the Concero brand (and our personal brands) to unimaginable new heights. Thanks to Kraig, the office energy is off the charts and the vibes from our workshop with him live on!"

—Jay Murchison, President & CEO, Concero

"It was a breakthrough day of high engagement and marked communication skill improvement that people are still talking about. He challenged our team to "step up and stand out" with what we say and why we say it. When the day ended, we all felt energized, unified, and more confident about ourselves as a team and as intentional communicators.

—Eric Kuester, V.P. Sales and Business Development, Pinehurst Resort

"His command of the room and the content he delivered was impressive beyond our expectation. Not only does Kraig possess valuable experience in executive communication and strategic marketing, his dynamic delivery and emphasis on storytelling and branding sets him apart from anyone I have seen present like this in a corporate forum."

—Mike Flaskey, CEO, Diamond Resorts

"We interviewed and discussed several highly sought-after public speaking/presence experts and made the unanimous decision to select Kraig. He connected personally with all our attendees, pushing them to modify and build on their strengths while developing new and differentiated skills. Our team members left energized and excited about immediately putting into practice what they had learned. Without a doubt, Kraig helped us "Elevate" our game!"

—Chris McManus, Senior Managing Director, Accenture

"Kraig Kann is a master communicator who engages and enlightens audiences the moment he steps on stage. Kraig weaves personal stories that are applicable with easily digestible lessons...leaving each person with a roadmap for success in building their own brand."

—Duane Cummings, CEO, The Sensational Group

"The whole sales team walked away inspired by Kraig's storytelling sessions and how he framed the opportunity to influence people into advocacy for the Titleist brand. The time in his "Elevate Workshop" has had a major impact on their ability to influence our accounts and dedicated golfers.

—John Screen, Vice President U.S. Sales, Titleist

"Kraig's keynote delivery was world class and his "Elevate Workshop" brought us closer as a team and was an amazing forum for us to share our backgrounds that otherwise could never have happened."

—Terry McCafferty, President & CEO, Falls Lake Insurance Companies

"In the insurance business, reputation and ability to communicate are critical to our success. The work Kraig did with our team helped them understand key concepts and strategies for delivering these skillsets in a more effective manner. I would encourage anyone to walk the steps with him."

—Peter Doyle, Regional President, Arthur J. Gallagher

"In the past, we've always focused our training efforts on sales process, rather than the personal side of presenting our ideas and personal roles to support the company. The team's feedback on Kraig's communications and public speaking workshops far exceeded our expectations and there was most certainly a buzz going through our office as he helped us #elevateWight."

—Bradley Paulsen, AIA, Sr VP, Chief Development Officer, Wight & Company

"Kraig's ability to get our team focused on the concepts of common messaging; everyone sells (all the time), and "stand-out when you stand-up," was exceptional. I was especially pleased with his constructive engagement of those executives who are not always in front of customers and/or prospects; helping them to get comfortable delivering the AdvantEdge message in their own unique voice."

—David H. Langsam, President & CEO, AdvantEdge Healthcare Solutions

"I have seen who I consider to be the best speakers in the country; Anthony Robbins, Ed Foreman, Zig Ziglar, Les Brown, Tom Peters and Stephen Covey. Some were great entertainers and motivators, while others were business methodology zealots. If you've seen Kraig Kann speak, teach, interact and perform then you know this guy can't be contained by a 5-star rating. As a former Dale Carnegie instructor, I recognize a talent in others being able to engage an audience. He's a freakish combination of C-Suite strategist and television entertainment."

—Jon Newsome, CEO, Presentation Partners

"Kraig absolutely, positively knocked it out of the park, challenging everyone to "get comfortable with being uncomfortable" while driving home the importance of "effective brand messaging." In a follow up survey, he received unquestionably the highest rating we have ever seen. While I certainly went into the sessions with high expectations of what he could help us accomplish, those expectations were exceeded in many ways."

—Mike Elliott, President, Golf - Greg Norman Collection & Dunning Golf

"I saw Kraig Kann speak at SAP's national, annual marketing meeting. He delivers energy and passion on stage comparable to Tony Robbins and Richard Branson. Kraig's simple, yet powerful methods engage audiences to self-reflect, create, and accelerate their communication skills. I would highly recommend you invite Kraig to speak, train and inspire your leaders to be their best selves!

—Melissa Lamson, CEO, Lamson Consulting

"Kraig always looked at the bigger picture to strategically position the LPGA Tour to maximize the exposure that we as players get. He really helped me to become more comfortable in dealing with and presenting to the media. It was like having a PR coach that was always available to help and support me, and also guide me in how to communicate to the media and ultimately to the viewers.

—Lydia Ko, LPGA Tour Major Champion

"It seems everything Kraig touches compellingly breaks through clutter, moving people to move needles. He is an "idea factory" rooted in programming that is specific, measurable, attainable, realistic and timely. I know first-hand because our firm was on the front line of Kraig's blend of traditional and unconventional thinking, and he helped unlock a lot of latent talents."

—Rich Katz, Founder, Buffalo Agency

"When I reached my forties, I was looking for a transition from playing full-time on the PGA TOUR. TV commentary was intriguing and I needed to set myself apart. Kraig excels because he evaluates what each person or business uniquely needs, tailors his consulting to help them improve. I'd recommend him and Kann Advisory Group to anyone looking to be a more polished presenter or finding a way to set themselves apart in their industry."

—Mark Wilson, 5-time PGA TOUR Winner

"Kraig Kann knows how to draw in an audience. His energy is sincere and I found myself feverishly writing down inspirational quotes and messaging to use in the future! His tenure in the business compliments his passion for teaching the fundamentals of communications while also highlighting the demands and value of social relevancy."

—Gina Lehe, Managing Director Communications,
Strategy & Branding, NCAA

"I've had the privilege of hearing many outstanding speakers over the last 30 years, however, I don't believe that any one of them has delivered a more powerful and thought-provoking message than the one Kraig Kann presented during the 2017 CoSIDA Leadership Forum. He draws from a wide-range of professional experiences to share a message that will leave you better both professionally and personally in today's ever-changing communications world."

—Nick Joos, Deputy Athletics Director & CCO,
University of Missouri Athletics

"Kraig's ability to inspire and guide our teams through his unique and motivating program over two days was remarkable. An eye-opener for everyone. Over the years, we have had several leadership sessions, and this one hands down, provided the content and connection for my sales team to bring out the best in our people."

—Tom Thomson, President & CEO, SCI Lighting Solutions

"Kraig's session was a highlight of our program. He captured and inspired the audience with a dynamic and engaging presentation, reinforcing the power of influence and the art of personal branding. "Creating that emotional connection" in communication resonated powerfully with our team. Kraig's expert advice, including helpful tools and actionable instructions, is a critical ingredient in developing our people and creating a world-class marketing organization!"

—David J. Hutchison, Former Senior VP & GM Marketing, SAP

"The energy and passion he brought to the topic of Personal Brand was exactly what we needed to energize our professionals. Through his professional experience as a network broadcaster and communications leader at the LPGA, Kraig provided valuable insights and advice, as well as an appreciation that in today's 24/7 communications environment, being able to cut through the noise and distinguish one's organization and one's personal professional brand has never been more challenging. His engaging, passionate and thought-provoking presentation and interactive session left us with important messages for today's communications professionals. He helped us build a better team culture in the process."

—Chris Monteiro, Former Chief Communications Officer, KPMG

Can You Get Our Attention?

STAND OUT
THE STORY
THE COMPANY
THE BRAND
YOU

KRAIG KANN

Headline Books, Inc.
Terra Alta, WV

Can You Get Our Attention?
Stand Out, The Story, The Company, The Brand, You

by Kraig Kann

copyright ©2021 Kraig Kann

All rights reserved. No part of this publication may be reproduced or transmitted in any other form or for any means, electronic or mechanical, including photocopy, recording or any information storage system, without written permission from Headline Books, Inc.

To order additional copies of this book or for book publishing information, or to contact the author:

Headline Books, Inc.
P.O. Box 52
Terra Alta, WV 26764
www.HeadlineBooks.com

Tel: 304-789-3001
Email: mybook@headlinebooks.com

ISBN 13: 9781951556518

Library of Congress Control Number: 2020949711

PRINTED IN THE UNITED STATES OF AMERICA

This book is dedicated to my parents, grandparents, brother, and most importantly, my children. Each of you have loved, inspired and supported me in your own special way. For all that you have given to me, I hope this becomes a special gift for you.

Allan -
Enjoy the book
and keep finding ways to
STAND OUT.
Share your story and, most importantly,
"get people's attention."

All My Best,

#ELEVATE

Table of Contents

Foreword

Don't wait for people to take notice. Do something positive that's worthy of people's attention.

When I was a young kid, I spent a lot of time walking to the local library and checking out books. I would grab two or three at a time and sometimes more. I had to return them in two weeks and I'd read them lying on my bed in my room in suburban Chicago. As I read, I thought about someday writing my own book. At that time, I had no idea what it would be about and I certainly didn't have an idea about who the book would serve.

During the summer between my junior and senior year of high school, I attended a leadership camp through my church. Among the things we were asked to do was compile a list of dreams for our life and to create a list of goals we'd like to achieve by the age of thirty. A book was among the first things I put on my list.

The problem with creating a list at the age of seventeen that includes a book, is you have no idea what direction your life will truly take, who will be in it with you, and what your career path might become. Heck, you don't even know where it will get started.

What makes one a good author? Why would anyone want to read what you have to say in the first place? What is my expertise?

Back then, I didn't know the answers to those questions. But here's what I know now.

Writing a book, while a lofty goal, is out there for anyone who puts their mind to it and is passionate about *something*.

Each of us has our own story to tell. Our stories can help others.

For me, what has always separated great authors is their creative and authentic ability to deliver a combination of stories and messages that positively impacts people. It's what you have to say that will positively impact others.

It's taken me a few years to write this book. The fact that my career has taken a few planned and unexpected turns has cemented my belief that I can aspire to help others believe in the power of themselves. Some people can be afraid to share the details of their life. I'm not that person and I never have been. I've pretty much always been an "open book." Those who know me best would no doubt agree with that. So now, it's time to write one. I hope you will enjoy it.

I'm a broadcaster by trade. I've spent more than twenty-five years in television, including an amazing and forever-rewarding eighteen years at The Golf Channel. I'm a communications executive by opportunity. I switched lanes abruptly and spent more than five years at the Ladies Professional Golf Association as its Chief Communications Officer. I'm a consultant by choice. My business - the Kann Advisory Group – and my careers, help me deliver something unique to people from all walks of business and sports. I'm an entrepreneur by birth. My mind has always raced with ideas and somehow during my career, I've been able to manage the fear of people telling me something wouldn't work out. I've also been able to manage the anxiety that often comes with thoughts of what others would, might or do think of me.

I'm proud of every single thing I've done in my career. Some things I never saw coming and I've re-invented myself on more than one occasion. I have learned that our career is always just an opportunity, person, or event away from abruptly changing course. And sometimes, your gut is what signals the time for something different. I hope this book will help you feel the same way about your professional path. I believe growth comes from every change and every new opportunity.

This book will deliver two things; the knowledge I've gained and the knowledge I've shared in my workshops, webinars, and keynotes. In doing so, I will focus on some key areas; each plays a key role in building a brand worth sharing and a brand that others will talk about. Not all of them will apply directly to you. But success with each will allow you to build your reputation and winning with each with give you an avenue to broadcast your story.

- Effective Communication
- Strategic Branding
- Presentation Skills
- Media Opportunities
- Media Relations
- Social Media Platforms

Throughout the book, you will learn the importance of building a personal and professional brand that's strong in the present and strong enough to keep you going when your career path changes direction.

You'll learn the value and critical importance of becoming a better presenter of yourself and you'll learn to better sell the brand(s) you represent. And I hope you'll become a believer that your own brand is real and worth spending time to build and time to share.

In addition to learning things to better take you down your own career path, I'll also present the personal story of my life and my career; how I got where I did, why I am where I am, and how the successes and disappointments can help you to become better than *you* thought you could be.

Along the way, I'll talk about the power that comes from *influence.* I'll share some words of wisdom from people who have been influential to me. You'll learn how they use their own *"voice of influence."* You'll understand why they mattered so much to me in my life, and perhaps it will spur you on to celebrating those who have left an important mark on you along the way.

Enjoy the read – I hope you'll find bigger value in yourself and a better idea of how to deliver for others in a way that takes you to your highest personal and professional summit.

CHAPTER ONE
What Else Ya Got?

Build a Second Something for YOU

The more you have to offer, the more attractive your brand becomes. The less you have to offer; the more anonymous your brand will remain.

I'm starting this book with something I never believed was all that important until I reached a point in my career where I thought I'd achieved my ultimate goal and was ready to settle in for the long haul. And then things began to change.

I learned that we all need to be prepared to adjust.

Life is full of curveballs. We throw ourselves curves along the way and others throw even bigger curves in our direction. No professional career is without a few plot twists.

Diversity in our personal and professional portfolio is a must. Security in our career of choice and loyalty from those who bring you onboard is not a given. Being great at something doesn't guarantee that *something* will always be there for you.

We must adjust.

From the time we are young, we realize eventually we will need to have a job. For some, it takes a long time to figure out what that job or career will be. Some go to school with a singular focus on what we want to do and what we will be. We put tons of effort into learning our craft and building our skillset to achieve great things and become the best we can become.

You may want to be an architect, a financial planner, a sales executive or sports executive, or maybe an accountant or a doctor. Or maybe your chosen destiny is to become a professional athlete. All are fine professions and many of them are lucrative beyond what we thought was possible.

Or maybe you want to become a news anchor or a sportscaster.

As you will learn in this book, I was dead set on a career in front of the camera, under the lights, and within the confines of a television studio or booth inside an arena or a big college or professional stadium. Along the way, I've learned that life changes and we change.

And the question becomes, "Can you adapt?"

Is there something else out there that will move you in a new direction? Is your passion pulling you away from your chosen path and pointing you toward something that moves you?

As I climbed through the local television markets and into the world of network cable television, I realized that I couldn't just be a *reader* or a host or a reporter. I needed other skills and I learned quickly that relationship building was going to be at least as important as being able to quarterback a thirty-minute show and stay on time while producers and directors were talking - sometimes yelling - in my ear.

The longer I stayed in television, the more I thought about what else was on the other side.

Some of my close friends were top salespeople. Others were executives for big corporations who traveled each week to exciting places – or so it seemed. And a few of my friends were climbing the ranks in the sports industry, working for teams or leagues and interacting with coaches, athletes and owners.

From the time I can remember, my head has always been on a swivel. My mind was always spinning on overdrive with thoughts about all the things you can do and what it takes to be successful.

If you're an ideas person, write them down as they come to mind. You'll never remember it the same way later.

So, I guess what I have done since the beginning of my professional career is to multi-task. I've taken a lot of mental notes along the way about learning new things and seeing what else might be possible and whether or not it might be a good fit for me. I wanted to be prepared because, as someone I valued a lot in my life once told me, "There is an expiration date on everything, including life itself."

You can't just be a one-trick talent.

As I look back now, I realize the value of a business degree even though I majored in journalism. I wish I had graduated with a double-major or at least minored in sports business or some level of business. It would be helpful to me in many ways.

I would tell anyone to grab some experience with smart businessmen and women who have created corporate or small business plans and led brands and people to greater heights.

I would emphasize the importance of learning how to sell. The skill it takes to persuade others to buy into what you are offering and the best way to negotiate for yourself and others has proven to be valuable to me along my career journey.

I paid close attention to the television industry and my eyes were wide open at all times. It didn't take long to realize that even the best in television don't last forever. People's value often lies in Q-ratings or the Q-score, which directly ties to familiarity and appeal for an audience. That doesn't even take into consideration expiring contracts or management change or whether the current executive fancies you as much as the prior executive did.

Ask yourself what else you can do. What would happen if?

And don't do it when you are fifty. Start thinking about building your skillset when you're twenty-five or thirty years old. Also, never minimize the importance of networking – and not just inside your chosen industry. Meet people who do things of interest to you. Learn what they do and how they do it.

I've been a videographer, a news reporter, a sports reporter, a sports anchor, a TV and radio play-by-play host, a radio talk show host, a sports executive, a communication head, a consultant, a leadership trainer, a media trainer, a board member, a faculty member and guest lecturer, keynote speaker, a podcaster, and now an author.

Trust me when I say that in moving into and through each of those career avenues, there was a strong degree of nervousness. I like trying new things and when opportunities came my way, more often than not, I said, 'yes.' My advice is that you do the same.

The key to building a lasting brand is to construct your resume with experience that ties together and keeps you moving in the right direction toward your career goal or goals, understanding they might change. Make sure to spread your wings where it makes sense and push yourself into new areas because you never know when you'll need the skillset to separate yourself from another qualified candidate.

Don't wait until it's too late.

KRAIG'S LIST

3 THINGS: I Hope You'll Learn In This Book

BIG VALUE IN YOUR BRAND & STORY: Don't shy from building and sharing to influence.

TOP PRESENTERS WIN: Where and how well you present you is more important than ever.

CAREER PIVOTS ARE "GO OPPORTUNITIES": Always build new skills. Always remain open to new challenges. Always ready yourself.

KANN LEADERSHIP

CHAPTER TWO

The Importance of YOUR Story

Why YOU Need to Know It and Why YOU Need to Own It

To build your story, spend time and shake yourself to your own core. Figuring out what your background says, what your beliefs are, and what you stand for is your foundation and also where your brand begins.

If you've sat in on one of my workshops or seminars, you know what happens when I take the stage or step to the front of the room to start my presentation.

Somebody is getting called on to stand in front of the group.

I give them a simple task that ties to me, asking them a simple question. "I want you to address this audience," I say. "Please, tell who you are and why we should care."

It's amazing what can happen next.

Some will freeze and stare directly at me without so much as a word coming from their mouth. Others, stuck, will say, "Hmmm, that's a really good question." They'll struggle and remain frozen. Others are more comfortable and quickly say, "Okay, my name is…" and away they go. But not many; actually, very few.

As I tell them, I'm not putting them on the spot to embarrass them. I've done the same to CEO's, executives at every level, coaches, athletes, and students, too.

I do it to prove a point to the audience that most people don't have the answer to the simplest question about who they are and what value they bring to others.

I'm big into watching body language and some people instantly become uncomfortable with the situation and standing in front of others talking about who they are. A small few, based on my experience of doing this time after time, get excited about the spotlight and launch into a little talk about their journey and what they do.

The other reason I do this exercise? Instantly, everyone in the audience perks up and focuses. They realize there's a chance I also randomly pick them to come stand in front of the group. **I've got their attention!**

Everyone has a story. Everyone has value. Not everyone is comfortable with how to frame it or how to deliver it.

The interesting thing is that our personal story is the one thing we should be most comfortable in knowing, yet sharing it and talking about ourselves is not something we feel confident about because of how we'll be received. Nobody likes someone who's always talking about themselves, right?

You see, grabbing people's attention is a big challenge in a world where there is so much noise and many people seemingly in competition for air time.

The reality is that through effective storytelling, we connect. And owning the art of connection is our biggest way to influence others positively.

Try this exercise and answer the following questions.

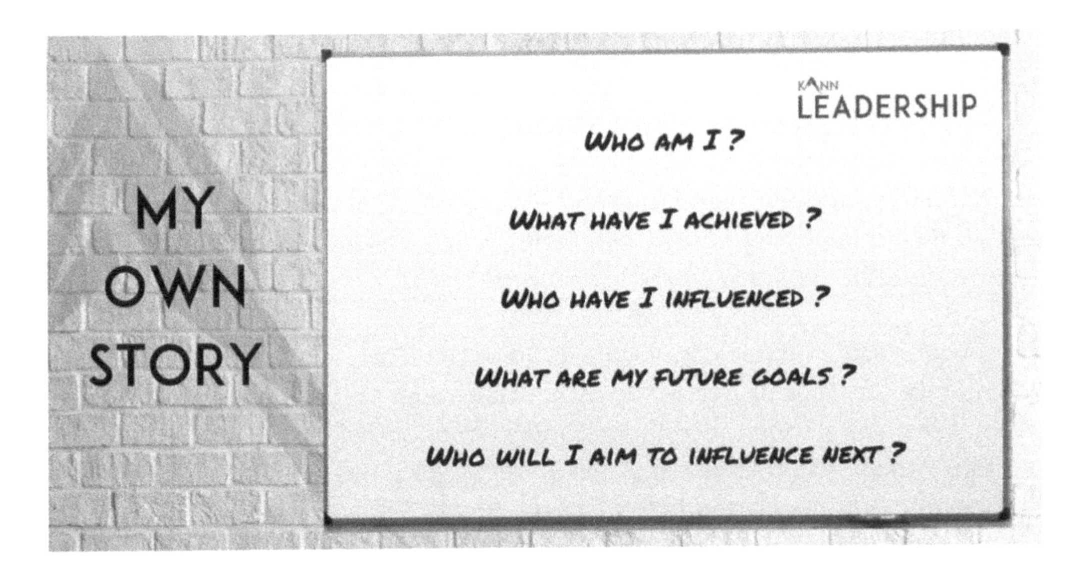

Before people buy a product, they buy the person selling it. We don't buy into something unless someone can convince us that there is something of value in it for us. Sometimes the best product isn't the product itself. It's the person telling us why it's great, why we need it, and what it will do for us.

Think about your experiences and the things you have done to get where you are. Think about what moves you've made and who's moved you to do one thing or another. That's part of your story.

One of my main goals with this book is to help you learn the importance of finding out your most important questions and then building your brand from those answers.

Every successful company goes through this exercise, figuring out who they are, what they do, why they do it and how they do it differently. The same must apply to each one of us.

If you asked me who I am, I would have a very quick answer for you.

"I'm an elevator." And with that answer usually comes a follow-up question like, "What do you mean?"

It's simple.

- I *elevate* people to become better.
- I *elevate* brands to become bigger.
- I *elevate* events to become grander.

In my workshops, designed to turn employees into ambassadors who can articulate the company story and sell it - I want people to think about the one word that best describes themselves. Once you have that singular word that best describes you, you are off to the races to explain to people your value. And once I understand your value and connect with you, I have a better chance to buy what you are selling.

Remember the question I ask people in my talks?

"Who are you and why should we care?"

It probably sounds a bit degrading. After all, asking someone why in the world we should care about them seems as though they probably aren't worthy of our attention. But actually, instead of asking, "Why we should care?" I could just as easily ask, "Who are you and why should we pay attention?"

Let's face it; there are a lot of people in this world. And no matter what we do for a living, there are plenty of others who do the same thing. We all need to find a way to stand out and separate ourselves from the crowd.

The easiest way to do that is through our story. Your story has great value. And if you learn to tell it effectively, and with compelling detail, you can connect with people, keep their attention and influence them to buy into what you're selling.

Master storytellers create legions of followers. Ask yourself if what you are sharing is so interesting or compelling that others will feel emotionally charged to pass it along.

I know for sure that nobody knows your story better than you. It's where your brand begins. And any successful brand requires knowing the story and having no fear of sharing.

The next time you get some time, think about how *you* can take the next step. Think about why storytelling can be so important for you. And, think about why learning to share your personal story and dynamically deliver it can be beneficial to those on the receiving end and build you a better future and career in the process.

MY STORY

A Chicago Kid with a Big Dream

The Room that Became My First Arena

My brand began before I ever turned ten.

How many people do you know who grew up on the same street? My family moved once during my childhood years but, believe it or not, we stayed on the same street! Two houses blocks apart on the same street. Woodland Avenue in Western Springs, Illinois, was the street I called "home."

I was born in LaGrange, which is a neighboring town in Chicago's west suburbs. Western Springs was the quaint, quiet town with elementary schools, a middle school, parks, courts and ballfields, tons of trees and a downtown with a train station and tracks that took many, including my dad on the commuter train to the big city for work each day.

My dad, Ken, grew up in the Chicago suburb of Oak Park and was an only child. He was a good athlete, playing quarterback on the football team, pitching on the baseball team and having a good run with basketball. My mom, Joanne, also spent much of her childhood in the Chicago area. She moved from Aurora, Colorado, before her teenage years and landed in the south suburbs. My dad was the dedicated, hardworking banker who ground it out day after day. He took the train every morning at about 7:15 and arrived home at about the same time each night, just after six. It drove me crazy that we didn't eat dinner as a family until about 7:15, but that was just the way it was. My dad was a man of routine and my mom was as good a homemaker as there was.

My brother, Brian, is two years younger, and we clashed as kids more often than not. We were nearly always at odds over loud music, privacy, and a few other things. It drove my parents nuts, but I don't know too many families who haven't lived that. Sibling rivalry in my house was probably a good reality television show that never made the air. Don't get me wrong, I love my brother and often promote him as one of the smartest people I know. We've each had our share of individual personal and professional challenges and leaned on

Kraig with brother Brian - Ft. Myers, FL

the other for support. We've had some bad moments as well that tie back to childhood in my opinion and I'm not proud of my part in that. But, to the best of my ability, I'd do anything for him and I'm pretty sure the feeling is mutual.

My house was a modest two-story home with four bedrooms. It had a large basement that had just enough room for a nerf basketball court my buddies and I turned into a makeshift arena where big games were played and plenty of sweat dripped. We played a lot. And being the creative kid, I hung pennants of my favorite colleges and professional teams around the walls down there to give it the best stadium feel I could.

But my bedroom was where it all started.

I was a sports freak at the earliest age with posters of all my favorite athletes, including basketball stars, George Gervin of the San Antonio Spurs and the great "Dr. J," Julius Erving. Football stars like Walter Payton of the Chicago Bears and Chuck Foreman of the Minnesota Vikings. Gervin and Foreman both wore number forty-four, my favorite number, and my first choice any time I got one playing basketball as a kid.

That bedroom had more posters and corkboard filled with pictures than you could imagine. And while I loved sports as much as any kid in the city, my goal wasn't centered around reaching the NBA or the NFL. My dream was to be a sportscaster.

Kraig's Dream Born at an Early Age

Yes, I wanted to be a sportscaster. And I was determined to find my way to a career with a microphone.

I can't tell you how many nights I spent under the sheets with the lights out, listening to my transistor radio. The White Sox, Blackhawks, and Bulls were the focus on many a night. I listened to the calls of announcers like Harry Caray, who was a member of the Sox broadcast team before he ever switched sides of town and joined the Cubs where he became a legend. Pat Foley has forever been a star voice for the Hawks. I remember WIND-AM in the 1980s like it was yesterday. Tony Esposito in goal, Keith Magnuson, and the great Stan Mikita ruled the Windy City at Chicago Stadium long before Patrick Kane and Jonathan Toews ever hit the ice at the United Center.

As for the Bulls, Jim Durham was my broadcast idol as a kid. He had amazing skills as a storyteller on radio. He made you feel like you were right inside Chicago Stadium and it seemed that every call of a missed shot included a "rimming.... no." Chet Walker, Bob Love, Jerry Sloan, Norm Van Lier, Artis Gilmore, and others were my childhood hoops heroes and much of it I credit to Durham, who also worked as the voice of the Dallas Mavericks and later joined ESPN where he became a household name. In my household, he was special. And I caught as many games as I could from underneath the sheets of my bed until my Mom or Dad figured me out and put curfews on my listening habits relegating me to a kid who usually missed out on the fourth quarter or the third period!

Guys like Durham gave me the inspiration to have my own voice. And beginning at about the age of seven or eight, I had my own tape recorder and microphone. And I was calling my own Bulls games and turning my bedroom with the orange shag carpeting – yes, I had orange shag carpeting – into my version of a press row seat courtside at the Chicago Stadium.

Kraig's Childhood Home – Western Springs, IL

"Ten seconds left in the fourth, John Mengelt off the feed from Love. He shoots deep from the corner, and it's good! It's good! Bulls win! Bulls win! 103-102!" I would shout. And on I would go, "We're back with the post-game show and my guest Reggie Theus - live from Chicago Stadium right after this time out. Bulls basketball is brought to you by Pepsi, so stay with us every one, I'm Kraig Kann and we're back right after this!"

My friends would come over and hope to join in when I'd do made up playoff games and need an analyst. Neighborhood buddies like Ted Cox and my best friend from childhood Dave Wojick would get the opportunity to 'work alongside' as I handled the play-by-play. We had a ball doing it and I went to the mic as often as I could. It was more than my hobby. It was my dream.

I listened to every game I could with a strong ear about how they did it and what made them special. Someday it would be me and I'd remember I got my start on the second floor of a simple house on Woodland Avenue in a room with orange shag carpet.

That's what I told myself. I was determined to make it come true.

CHAPTER THREE
Effective Communication to Win

Why It's More Important Than Ever for YOU

Everyone gets distracted. Your job is to change their environment. Be someone whose words can make them excited to focus.

I once heard a line I've never forgotten. I share it in each of my talks and seminars.

Communication is the link between ideas and action.

Think about it. In its simplest form, isn't that correct?

Every meaningful relationship requires communication—friendships, dating, marriage, parenting, career, and on and on.

Each of us has things that swirl around and around inside our brain. Things we want to share. And with everything we think about, we often take the most important ideas or thoughts and share them with others.

But we don't just share to share. We share to deliver something in hopes of a response or a result. We share to make an impact or create a feeling inside someone else. We share with hope those on the receiving end will do something or feel something about what we say or with what we say.

Perhaps you've heard this before. If you've taken part in my communication workshops, you've heard it said more than once. And I repeat it to make sure people remember it.

There are a lot of people who talk. There are very few who actually say something.

These two sentences apply to our lives in more ways than we could possibly imagine.

Two types of communication stand out.

- **Written** – the skill of putting ideas and thoughts into words shared via paper, letter, email or text.
- **Verbal** – the skill of sharing ideas and thoughts in front of an audience, no matter how large or small.

Effective communication and thoughtful communication separate people. Thinking before we speak or thinking before we write can be the difference in delivering something that makes a positive impact or a negative impact.

If communication really is the link between ideas and action, then we sure better think about what we are saying and how we say it. And that means we'd better have a message. A real message.

The best message is one that is clear, concise, memorable, shareable, and repeatable.

In communication, the message isn't one of many things. It's where everything begins.

It's the only thing that matters. Because if you don't have a worthy message, then who's going to pay attention? Who's going to remember that it was you who delivered it in the first place? Who's going to care enough, or be emotionally charged enough, to share it with others?

Great communicators offer value and inspiration in their messages. If not, nobody remembers they were actually the communicator.

Building a brand requires creative and strategic communication. It requires you to have a worthy message. It requires you to know exactly what you are trying to convey and what you want the outcome to be.

I've been fortunate, to say the least, to be able to share my story as a way of helping others learn to deliver their own. It bears repeating that the art of communication is a part of every walk of life. Personal and professional relationships, career growth, dealing with children, coaching, etc. require putting your best words forward.

Just like every corporation or organization has a brand story and a message they'd like to get into the mainstream, so, too, should every person and every employee have their own clear, authentic message within their story or line of communication.

Ask yourself these questions:

- What stands out about me personally that I can trace to my childhood?
- What stands out about me professionally that adds value to my organization?
- Am I a thought leader and someone who commands attention when I speak?
- Can I add value in a company meeting with something on the line?

I love the idea of creating ideas. I always have. But the true challenge is making something great from the good ones. That means being able to communicate your thoughts and ideas effectively and then getting them across the finish line. The most influential people know just how to do this. At work, it's a big separator.

Remember, we influence by getting people to connect with us. So, just like creating and building a corporate brand requires identifying what makes it unique and fascinating, building a personal and professional brand means identifying what makes ***you*** unique and fascinating.

If you're looking for an edge over those in your office or your industry, you'd better be able to elevate your skills and take on the fear of being uncomfortable when speaking or selling.

The same applies to us in our time away from work. We want to be received in the best way possible, right? So, before you speak or before you write, think about what you'll say and how it will be received.

Have you spent time thinking about your message?

Here's an exercise for you before you head into your next week.

With regard to work, consider the idea or concept you want to get across for the coming week. Put it on paper. Analyze it. Then spend some time thinking about how you'll get the message across. Will you send out an email within the company? Will you hold a meeting with your team?

If you work for yourself and run your own business, consider what you want customers (your audience) to know about your company at this exact moment. How will you get the message out? Is it a single post on social media? Is it a video you can shoot and produce that will be put onto your website? Is it a new campaign you can put into motion to engage your audience?

The same goes for family. Perhaps you've been thinking about the successes of your children at school or in their various sports, but didn't know how to put your thoughts into words. What will you do and how do you want them to feel? What will your message be and how do you want it to be received? Those are the questions we should ask.

Without the ability to put our thoughts into words, we are left with an overload of information that can, at times, be overwhelming and confusing. The best communicators can narrow the focus, figure out the main message to deliver and then spend time figuring out how to get the message across in the most effective way.

Start thinking about how you present every big message you have. The way you do it and the way you make people feel ties directly to your brand. What people think and what people say links back to how you present yourself and your ideas.

People take the idea of communication for granted. I say it's time to start putting more effort into what you put out there.

If you want to win with your story, think about every way you'll communicate it. I think you'll get some favorable results.

KRAIG'S LIST

3 THINGS: Keys To An Effective Message

CONCISE AND CLEAR: Not too long and certainly to the point.

MEMORABLE: Lot's of people talking. Make sure you actually say something.

SHAREABLE: Clear and memorable equals repeatable. Work to inspire further conversation.

KANN LEADERSHIP

CHAPTER FOUR

Effective Communication to Win

Getting YOU the Edge on Your Competition

In communication, the more detail you offer, the more impactful the message. The less you offer, the less chance anyone remembers you were the communicator.

I say it a lot. Ordinary doesn't work. If we want to become a brand worth following, we need to strive for extraordinary in everything we do.

When it comes to communication, ordinary doesn't get you noticed. In fact, you'll be forgotten.

I once had the pleasure to speak to more than seventy-five communication executives from powerhouse brand KPMG in New York City as part of a team-building communications conference. I was super excited and honored to share my experience.

I was on stage about three hours motivating and empowering some of the best and brightest in the corporate world to think differently and rise to new personal and professional growth levels.

I was asked to speak about "executive presence" -- finding your way to the C-Suite and how communication can be such a valuable tool in your professional tool kit. As I said earlier, those who've seen my keynotes in person know that I love to put the audience to the test in a few ways. I enjoy engaging them and helping them understand the importance of their value and personal and professional story.

Again, I called a few people to the stage to join me and ask them, "Who are you and why should we care?"

People don't usually feel comfortable talking about themselves, which is understandable. But we need to find a way to get over it, and we need to do it in a hurry.

If you want to be the best at something, stand out in a crowd, or rise within an organization or industry, you'd better understand yourself and be able to promote your value.

According to the Carnegie Institute of Technology, "85% of your financial success is due to your personality and ability to communicate, negotiate and lead. Shockingly, only 15% is due to technical knowledge."

So what does that say? It says that public speaking and presentation skills should never be taken for granted.

If you're looking for an edge or a raise, you'd better find a way to elevate your skills and take on the fear of being uncomfortable when speaking or selling.

Is your communication message worthy? If not, it's probably just somebody's spam. Make sure you're actually saying something.

To me, the greatest skill a leader can possess is owning communication. Leadership isn't just in the form of a job title on a business card. It's a way of doing things and engaging and empowering others to become their best.

I've been around some really good leaders, a couple I consider to be great leaders. And I've been around a few who I am surprised were ever given the opportunity to control the destiny of an organization or its people. You've probably seen the same. We learn from all of it.

While leaders have their own individual style, people who follow make choices about just how much enthusiasm they will have about their job and their leader based on many things. But above all, I think, is the leader's style and – get this – their command of communication.

In my mind, it boils down to this:

People choose to **L**isten

People choose to **E**ngage

People choose to **A**ct

People choose to **D**eliver

A leader's communication style greatly influences the degree to which everyone in an organization or on a team will follow along and become a motivated and inspired employee or team member. How much they share, how they share it and how they make you feel while sharing it plays a part in a leader's degree of effectiveness.

How many times have you said, or thought to yourself, "I don't really know what's going on around here?" Or perhaps someone has said, "Do you understand the goal or the mission? Help me, because I sure don't."

During my time as the LPGA's Chief Communication Officer, I made it a regular practice to sit with those on our team to share thoughts about what we were doing, how we should be doing it and why we were doing it. I tried to give teammates every opportunity to talk to me about their role and also allow them to challenge me where they felt necessary to help make us better.

We had an amazing team and each one of them learned to understand the importance of having a message and making sure they shared it effectively with others.

We all need to be sharp with our message. We need to deliver a clear understanding of what is expected and we can never give people enough encouragement or feedback – even if it's not what someone wants to hear. I've certainly benefitted from the feedback over the years.

One of the companies I have worked with through Kann Advisory Group is an architecture and design firm named Wight & Company. They are based in Chicago. During our two days of workshops, the focus and mission was to take their professionals who plan, design and deliver new buildings or transform space inside existing structures, and make them more comfortable and more engaging at presenting and pitching in front of prospective clients or communities.

Like any company, some were more comfortable in the moment than others. But some stood out from the moment they got their first opportunity in front of the group. It's one thing to be a skilled architect armed with a stack of impressive drawings or innovative plans. Where things get different is when the skilled architect becomes a dynamic entertainer who holds people's attention and can communicate the real reasons behind someone choosing their firm.

Most architects would not be imagined as engaging speakers. One who is, has a great ability to stand out among his or her peers. The level of their influence grows.

Success and climbing the career ladder for someone skilled at presenting and articulating their thoughts in the field of engineering or architecture is really no different from those I worked with in my years in broadcasting. Those who could engage and deliver a valuable message while holding the attention of an audience would rise above the others. Those who struggled to articulate and deliver with an energetic tone and cadence would be left behind. It's that simple.

We have to understand that everyone is talking these days. Every company has a message, and every employee has an audience at one point or another. Is your message better than someone else's? Can you truly grab an audience and then hold them? Can they remember what you've told them? Is it compelling enough that they'll share it with others?

If you can succeed with those questions, you'll win almost every time. You'll also get noticed. Being a top communicator is a great skill you can own. If you want an edge on the competition or a raise – be it financial or in brand stature – learn to own it.

Communication is more important than it's ever been.

If you want to win with your story, don't wait to make solid communication a priority. Put it at the top of your list. Your competitors and your co-workers will notice. And you'll stand out in every crowd.

KRAIG'S LIST

3 THINGS: Communication And Leadership

BE BELIEVABLE: The strength of the spoken or written word is tied to a platform of trust.

TARGETED MESSAGES: Who's listening? Only those you inspire to pay attention.

SAY WHAT?: Great leaders make you remember what you're supposed to remember.

KANN
LEADERSHIP

MY STORY

The Time That I Just Knew

Papers, Pictures and a Promise

Young and Motivated

I was the kid in grade school who had a lot to say and enjoyed finding any audience who'd give me the time of day to listen. Ask those on my neighborhood block or those in my elementary and middle school classes if I ever had a fear of raising my hand and they'd probably laugh.

While I like to say that I got my start in broadcasting before the age of ten from the confines of my bedroom with the tape recorder and microphone, I'd say that I got my start in marketing at about twelve or thirteen years old.

As a huge fan of all Chicago sports teams, I couldn't wait for my dad to get home off the train from the city with his newspaper. He was a fan of the Chicago Tribune and he read it on the commute home. I would wait, and when he got to the house, I would make it mine. I had zero interest in the front page or the lifestyle section. It was all about sports.

I could tell you about every team and every statistic. And I knew all the top athletes, from Bill Melton to Carlton Fisk on the White Sox, to Ryne Sandberg, Ron Cey and Andre Dawson on the Cubs. I didn't just know the great Bears running back Walter Payton. I knew all you needed on journeyman quarterback Bob Avellini too. And when the "Iceman" George Gervin somehow found his way from San Antonio to Chicago to play for the Bulls, I thought I'd gone to heaven. I loved the way he shot it and his finger roll was as good as it came.

It was during my middle school years that I just knew I wanted a career that had something to do with sports. But my mind also liked the business side of things. And I had a marketing plan that I was ready to put into action that covered both skills.

I determined that the *Chicago Tribune* needed some competition. And it wasn't going to come from the crosstown paper – *the Chicago Sun Times.*

I created the "Kraig Kann Sports Page." It was a hand-written, authentic gem of a journalism masterpiece.

It was a tedious process, compiling statistics from my favorite teams, and writing down the standings from all the leagues. My favorite part was the commentary. I'd have a "take" on almost everything and everyone. No team was exempt from my opinions and every team owner was at risk. I drew pictures too. Athlete sketches were one of my greatest passions. Sadly, I lost most of my collection when the treehouse my friends Ken Kramp, Dave Hutchison and I called our "second home" somehow caught fire and all the artwork I stored there was lost forever. We've never identified the culprit.

Anyway, I wrote about six or seven pages every week or so and then went down to the local Western Springs library - Thomas Ford Memorial – and made photocopies. I'd then staple it together and it was ready for delivery. Whether anyone in my neighborhood wanted it or not, they got a copy in the mailbox.

As you can see, I communicated at a "high level" before I ever made it my career.

I knew that's the way I'd make my living. I didn't know where, or with whom, or exactly how, but I knew that's what I'd be pushing for.

Kraig's High School – Lyons Township HS LaGrange, IL

This was all confirmed at a recent middle school and high school reunion weekend outside Chicago. A number of my running mates, who knew me back in the day, offered up stories about me rolling into basketball or football practice with an armful of sports pages, ready to share an earful of useless sports data! It was my passion and I was indeed THAT kid.

The older I got, the more I looked for opportunities to stand in front of an audience or put my name out there. As a high school student, I was given the opportunity to give the Sunday sermon for the entire congregation at my church as a part of Youth Sunday. I spent hours preparing and somehow nobody walked out of the sanctuary that morning.

I guess I was blessed with no fear and never had a doubt about what I would someday do. I had a whole lot of fun along the way.

If I could share one thing with kids today, it's the importance of conversation and communication. Not everyone will take the initiative to create a self-made newspaper or deliver a podcast, and I understand that. But sharing stories, engaging in conversation and having real dialogue with friends and adults, face to face, serves people well for years beyond their school grade.

Later in life, we are preached to about the importance of networking as a building block for future success.

Networking requires initiative and confidence, which isn't always comfortable for everyone. But pushing beyond self-created boundaries and putting yourself out there is a great thing in finding yourself, your voice and your purpose – even if you mess up a few times along the way. Gosh knows, I sure did.

By the time I'd hit the high school years, I was comfortable with who I was and where I wanted to go. That's when I started getting serious.

CHAPTER FIVE

Strategic Branding to Win

Think About It. Trust Me, It's Okay for YOU

Always remember, you are the Chief Marketing Officer of your brand. Build it with care, own it, deliver it with purpose.

The look on people's faces staring back at me says it all.

Be it a room of twenty during a leadership communication workshop, or an auditorium filled with several hundred, the minute I tell them they are a "brand" of major importance is the minute they start paying attention.

The concept of thinking of yourself that way can be uncomfortable. Certainly, we can't be equal to a product or corporation with their name in bright lights or the subject of a thirty-second commercial. Can we?

Yes. Yes. Yes.

Please hear this. Get over the idea that you aren't a big deal with the potential to impact people and make something bigger of yourself. You are. Make it your mission to do so and do it in a hurry.

It doesn't mean you're bragging about yourself. It means you're giving value to yourself. There's a big difference.

As a kid eagerly following sportscasters and play-by-play announcers, I recognized those who had a distinctive style or voice and a memorable delivery. I would try to copy them and I realized the great ones stood out for some reason or another and if I wanted to do the same, I had to have my own distinct style. I had to have my own way of being me. It was a must.

Whether it was being listed on the roster of disc jockeys at the high school radio station, in the mix with classmates at the television station on the University of Missouri campus, or trying to find my way from market to market in local news, the mission was the same. I quickly learned that I had to find a way to stand out. I had to have a certain "something" that would allow me to separate myself from others. That's what everyone was trying to accomplish. If you wanted an opportunity to show what you could do, you had to give them a reason to look your way. You had to be noticeable.

After all, certain commercials stick with you on television. Certain products are more recognizable on the shelves at the grocery store. And certain people draw more attention in the workplace. That's the reality. And it always will be.

I looked up the word "brand" one day in several searches. What showed up was dialogue about the process involved in *creating a unique name and image.* What stood out to me was the word ***unique.***

Personal brand doesn't just happen. It requires an acceptance that you are bigger than you think you are and believe your best success will come from devoting energy to doing things differently than others and delivering in a way that makes people take notice and share what you've delivered with others.

A light bulb needs to go off where you stop thinking about just doing things and start thinking about **how** you do the things you do, ways you can do them differently, and what you'll choose to put your energy toward.

If you want to be relevant in your industry, carve out your niche and focus your energy on doing relevant things that get noticed.

Take a few minutes and ask yourself how you got where you are. Trace your steps and see where the successes came from. Write them down. And equally important, discover where your failures pushed you. Write that down too.

The minute you don't value yourself as a brand – personally or professionally – is the minute you've cut your legs out from under you. You are admitting that you are plain old *ordinary.*

Any company that hires you or any team or organization that includes you needs you to add a unique value. They don't want you to simply blend in. They want something special from you that makes the team great and the others around you better. They want *extraordinary.*

I've hired my share of people and been part of plenty of group hiring processes during my career and I can promise you that at no point did we look to settle for a middle of the road employee.

I spent a lot of years during my career, trying not to rock the boat or do anything offensive to others. I figured if I could just be a solid contributor who fit the template my bosses were looking for, I'd find my way to great success. And for many years, my trajectory was on a northward path and I had the raises and the contract extensions to suggest I was doing the right thing.

What I heard from many of my executive bosses was that I was "good at many things" and "versatile" and "able to do everything." I was proud of that, yet I was never quite comfortable with just being a big part of the mix. I know that seems strange and I certainly wasn't chasing stardom. I was proud of being a part of a team of great talent.

Yet, I was hoping for a role I could call my own. Something where I could stand out and be known for something, instead of just being known for fitting into many things. I don't think I'm alone in having thought that along the way.

The idea of brand – to me – ties into the concept of carving out a niche for which you are recognized. Being an expert at something and having people call on you for the strength, knowledge, and experience in one area is a powerful calling card that will create a following and give you long-lasting relevance.

For a while, I guess I could say that my brand was about being versatile and reliable. That probably takes you a long way, but it doesn't sound really exciting.

My challenge to you is that you spend time thinking about what makes you, YOU.

Consider your strengths and the reasons people are drawn to you and the things that give you energy and opportunity to show passion.

Through this reflection, you might just find your exciting present and a future that gives you the greatest fulfillment you've ever had.

Ask yourself this; if I'm able to find what stirs something inside and creates an opportunity to shine like never before, would I drop what I'm doing and put more effort into taking that to a higher level? If the answer is yes, the time is now to think about the brand you are and the bigger brand you can become.

Now, try answering the following questions:

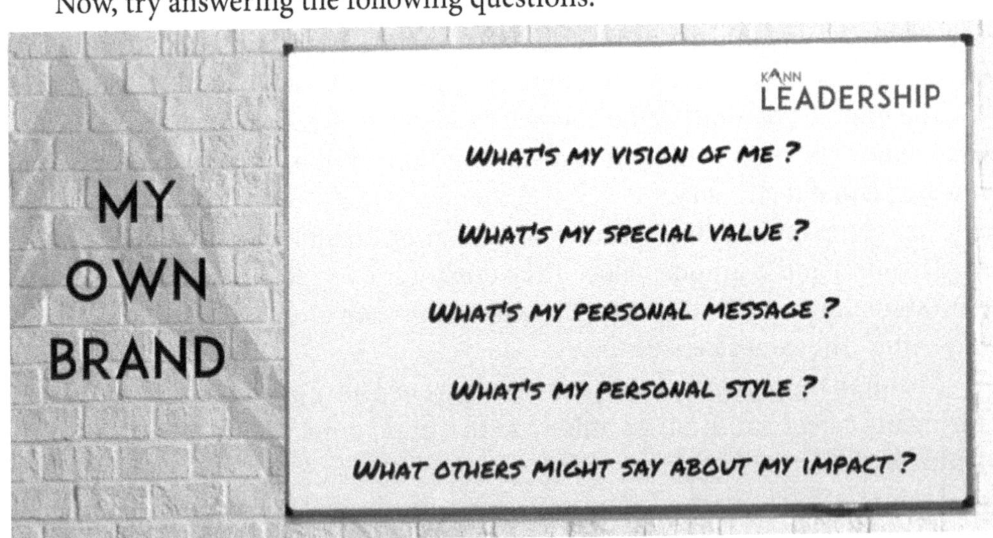

These questions are the foundation of personal brand. They don't answer the "what you'll do to stand out," but they will help answer the "who are you?" which is critical to understanding what makes you, YOU.

Fear not. It doesn't matter what you do for a living. This exercise applies to everyone and as you begin to find your true calling and the way you'll make a real difference, I promise it will help set the foundation for your personal and professional success.

If you want to win with your story, spend time considering yourself and the things people will enjoy hearing.

KRAIG'S LIST

3 THINGS: Key Personal Branding Qualities

AUTHENTICITY: Clarity in what you stand for and just being 'you.'

ENERGY: Passion for what you deliver and how you represent yourself.

SOCIAL CONNECTION: Ability to effectively engage others and create emotion.

KANN LEADERSHIP

CHAPTER SIX

Strategic Branding to Win

It Begins with a Mindset Owned by YOU

Forget what the job title on your business card says. At the beginning of the day, everyone can be an entrepreneur if they choose to be.

Do you remember the first business card you ever received with your own name on it? I remember getting a business card from WTVM-TV in Columbus, Georgia and feeling like I had truly arrived. It was my first job on my career journey and my first official business card. I was super excited.

As good as it felt, I was already thinking ahead to what my second card might say. That's not to say I didn't appreciate where I was. There is nothing like the first job to let you know you are on your way to establishing a career.

It took me a few cards and a few jobs to realize that there was always another card that might feel better and another job title that might make me feel more important.

In my time at The Golf Channel, my card went from Reporter/Anchor to just Anchor. That felt pretty cool. It required a lot of work and hours and challenges to prove myself an important part of such a talented team. But I was guilty of looking ahead to what might be next and what might make me feel more special about the role I had.

I remember being offered the role of Chief Communications Officer of the LPGA and thinking about the word "Chief." At first, I wondered if I was worthy because it was such a lofty title. That lasted for a while. I had such great respect for that title and all that went with it. It was a lot to live up to.

Yet, with my years of unique experience and the confidence that I could and would make a difference, I eventually grew comfortable with the title and felt like it was an okay fit. I know this, it certainly wasn't going to hurt my brand. The key was making sure I continued to deliver on the expectations that went with the title. People counted on me and I expected a lot of myself.

My point in sharing is that many of us look at the title we are given more than the opportunity that comes with the role. We are often caught focusing energy on the goal of promotion ahead of the goal of production. We attach unneeded worth in the title bestowed upon us when we are hired and spend unneeded time working to achieve the next title on the career ladder. I admit to falling into that mindset at times.

I hired multiple people during my time with the LPGA. On many occasions, candidates would come into the interview with sights set on the next job they might get within the organization rather than the job we were discussing. I could feel it.

In other words, a candidate was looking to be a senior manager before spending time in the role of manager. I had a few, who during annual reviews, were focused more on the title change they were chasing than listening to me share the great things they had done and the raise they were about to receive.

While I don't fault anyone for working toward and thinking about career advancement, I believe that we'd be a lot better off if business cards didn't have titles associated with names.

What we do means a lot. How we do what we do and how we tell people what we do means a lot more in building a brand.

Brands are about the people and what they deliver, not the title.

And if having a title is a must, then I'd go with the title "Entrepreneur."

Entrepreneurs are risk-takers. They get up in the morning focused on achieving a goal and they have a bold confidence in their ideas and beliefs. A successful entrepreneur looks at the potential outcome of greatness, not the potential pitfalls that might come along the way to producing something others will discuss.

Each of us has a gift. Each of us has an inner genius about something. It's our job to go chase it without fear.

I believe it doesn't matter if your business card says coordinator, manager, senior executive, or CEO. For that matter, having "intern" next to your name should be just as empowering. The opportunity just to be a part of something with the chance to make a name for ourselves should be what drives us.

Our primary ambition should be to deliver something special and have something attached to your name that provides value and emotional connection to others.

Some people say that "brand" is just a fancier word for reputation. Perhaps that's true. But, to me, brand means something larger. Brand suggests that you stand for something, represent something and not just that you are something. Each leads other people to have a conversation. Reputation gives off a direct link to gossip and chatter. Brand will give people an immediate idea about what you might provide or inspire in others. Brand suggests that you are known for something and quite good at something.

On your next Monday morning, wake up with a new mindset and consider yourself an entrepreneur. Promise yourself you'll attack the day with a vision for doing something bigger than the norm and something more than what might be expected. In being *you*, give people a fearless person who's ready to take an idea and make it great.

That's what entrepreneurs must do each day.

If you want to win with your story, carry yourself like an entrepreneur. Own your ideas, own your story and own your brand. I think you'll like the feeling it gives you.

KRAIG'S LIST

3 THINGS: Top Traits For Top Professional Brands

EXECUTIVE PRESENCE: Own the room. Own the audience. Own the moment.

CONTROL AND COMPOSURE: Ready and impressive when others are stressed.

PREPAREDNESS: Ability to see what's coming before it hits. Never caught looking.

KANN LEADERSHIP

MY STORY

My High School Days

College Prep that Began with a Shock

I attended Lyons Township High School in La Grange, Illinois. For years, it has been one of the state's largest public schools. The campus felt more like a college than a high school. There were two campuses actually – it was **that** big. Freshmen and sophomores attended class on the school's south campus and juniors and seniors hit the books about a mile away at the north campus.

To describe me in high school would be interesting.

I would suggest that I was a B-plus student with an A-track brain focused on my future. I played three sports almost every year of my high school career and found my way into the school radio station - WLTL 88.1 on your FM dial - where I did a variety of things, including DJ, talk and news updates. It was an opportunity most schools don't offer. At least not back in the early 1980s!

Three teachers stood out and truly made an impact on me. Jack Wiesemes, Kate Singletary and Dennis Strecker were the primary faculty members running the station. They volunteered their time and ran the studio while we were trying to soak it all in and find our way. It's where I got my legitimate first start. It was a big step up from the orange shag carpeting in my bedroom, where I'd been broadcasting my own games.

Strecker was special for me. He was my math teacher too—poor guy. Math was never my thing – my three kids will attest to that as they always ran to their mom for help in that area. Strecker drew my name for Geometry, which was the only math class I considered to be of any use because I could draw things. But more than that, he saw something in me as a young broadcaster and we've stayed in touch to this day.

I played football all four years. I wasn't great, but I found my way into the starting line-up on the offensive line each of my first two years. With more than a hundred kids out for the team, that was no small task. Junior year was a disappointment and senior year started great but I lost my starting job to a junior who – quite frankly – was tougher and better.

Oddly enough, I was the team's punter as well. And I was good at it.

I can pretty much guarantee I was the only punter in suburban Chicago who wore number sixty-two, played offensive line and then dropped back on fourth down to punt. I found my way onto the all-conference and Chicago all-area teams my senior year thanks to a few great games and being pretty consistent.

We were good.

Highly ranked, we found our way into the state quarter-finals before losing at home without our three best players due to injury. Our coach was Dick Wojick and he was like a second father to me growing up because his middle son happens to be my best friend. Dave Wojick was our quarterback and recruited by many schools until a horrific injury derailed his senior year about four games into the season.

A junior named Steve Peake took the reins and was solid, if not spectacular, under the circumstances. To this day, I think we all wondered what would have happened had Dave not been tackled on a run that resulted in a broken arm sending him to the hospital for immediate surgery.

Football was fun. I spent a few years on the baseball team as well. But basketball was my dream sport.

I spent my junior high days playing every day and shooting until dark. I wasn't blessed with jumping ability or speed. But I could shoot it well, and I considered myself a darned good passer. I thought basketball was my calling.

And that's where everything took a strange turn.

Senior Year High School Football

A week before freshman basketball tryouts, I sprained an ankle, and the timing couldn't have been worse. With a large high school, there was a freshman "A" team and a freshman "B" team. Coaches knew me from camps and I had achieved success in junior high where basketball in our area was a really big deal and league games after school were must-attend events for fellow students, parents and others in the area.

That said, my basketball tryout wasn't bad. But I wasn't at my best.

After tryouts, the names were posted on the wall for everyone to see. I don't remember how many kids made the roster, but I remember staring at the sheet for what seemed like hours without seeing my name.

Something had to be wrong.

My name wasn't there.

No matter how long I looked and from which direction I stared, I couldn't find it.

I was in shock.

I remember it like it was yesterday because of the number of kids who came up to me as confused as I was. The ride home that night with my buddy Dave Wojick, another kid and Dave's mom who had the carpool that night, was painful. I don't think I said a word and I know that they certainly didn't know what to say to me.

When I got home, I went straight to my room and cried. I couldn't get the visual of the piece of paper taped to the wall - without my name – out of my head.

As the story goes, I had a decision to make and I wasn't about to give up.

After a few days of self-pity mixed with anger, I joined my church basketball league and played with and against a bunch of kids who also fell short of their goals. It was pretty competitive, which was a blessing and made it worthwhile.

I still went to freshman basketball games to support my friends, which was hard. And I went to basketball camp the next summer with all the kids who had played on the freshman team.

I got cut again my sophomore year as the team had been whittled down from "A" and "B" to just one team.

Determined, I attended camps again. To be honest, my whole goal was just to **make** the team. And somehow, I did my Junior year. Perseverance had paid off, and I had my chance to be part of a highly ranked team in the state with players like Elmer Robinson, Dave Satek and Jeff Rochowiak on the team. To date, it was my proudest moment.

High School Gym with the Radio Booth Above

After a junior varsity season, I made the team again my senior year. But when we went to pick up our game jerseys before the season began, something else happened that I never saw coming.

While my favorite number was forty-four, that number was taken. I decided I would choose fifty-four, which was worn by Rochowiak the year before. I looked up to him and his toughness. But as I went to pick up the jersey from the table, the equipment manager told me, "you can't have it."

He reasoned that with fifteen players on the team, only twelve would dress for games. He told me and two others that we would be lumped among three who would rotate and dress out for one-third of the schedule.

Again, a crushing blow to my vision of a successful basketball career.

I went home that night and had another long talk with myself. And I came to a decision. A decision that would shape my future from that point on.

I went to practice the next day and asked legendary Chicago area coach Ron Nikcevich for a few minutes to talk on the court after practice.

Nikcevich was a legend in the state, a member of the Illinois Basketball Coaches Association Hall of Fame and the rare coach to lead a team to an undefeated season and a state championship in his first season with a school. His LaGrange team went 31-0 in 1970. He was a tall man, and a coach who stood tall in the eyes of every player who suited up for him.

I said, "Coach, I never have quit anything in my life, but I need to quit this team and it's certainly not easy, but I need to do it."

He asked why.

I told him I had an opportunity to be the play-by-play man for WLTL-FM and call games and with that being my future path, I thought it was best that I take the opportunity and run with it. I told him there was nobody who knew the team better and it was a way I could contribute while not being on the bench in a jersey.

Coach Nikcevich's words have never left me.

"I've had people quit before," he said. "But I've never had anyone quit with a real purpose."

He wished me well and told me he'd help in any way he could. And with that, I was off to set sail on my future.

I partnered with Phil LeBeau. Phil was an ambitious young broadcaster and, like me, would end up attending the University of Missouri for a future in broadcast journalism. His career has taken off as he is in the NBC network news family as a reporter covering automotive and aviation news.

We had a blast and I still have the cassette tapes of our calls during the 1983-84 season.

While I played football, caught behind the plate on the varsity baseball team and ultimately had a cup of coffee on the basketball team, my greatest success in high school came from my failure.

My success was finding my real calling at a younger age than most. Not making the team I dreamed of became the launching pad for a mindset that has served me well for years. I believe that once you know what you want to do, take aim at the plan to get there. Bumps in the road are just that. Stay in your lane and drive forward.

As I tell people, the writing was literally on the wall after my freshman basketball tryout.

It just took me a few years to figure out what I was meant to do. And I'm truly proud of what I went through and how I got there. And by the time I crossed the stage at graduation – ironically inside the basketball gym – I was already well on my way to a broadcasting career.

Senior Year High School Yearbook

CHAPTER SEVEN
Presentation Skills to Win

Let Anxiety Help YOU

Standing in front of people is your opportunity. Standing out when you get the chance becomes your brand.

Have you ever been awarded the task of standing in front of your co-workers and sharing your team or organization's successes? Or maybe you've been asked to present a plan that the team or organization is ready to launch?

Alone?

With nobody by your side?

If you've never done it before, you'll undoubtedly encounter a jumbled mess of nerves, butterflies, and anxiety swirling around in your head – and your stomach.

Know this; the minute someone leans on you to represent the thoughts or ideas of others, or challenges you to present your own, is the minute you've been given a gift.

That's right. It's a gift.

Some people in your office or your industry will never get that golden opportunity. They are relegated to being in their office or cubicle without the chance to present something of meaning.

Among the many ways you can separate yourself from competition in your chosen field—the best way I can think of is being tagged as "above average" to "great" as a public speaker or presenter.

People notice you. They remember you. They will talk about you.

I've spent most of my career presenting every day in front of a television audience with a degree of pressure to perform and deliver smoothly. People expect energy that makes the message, or the conversation, come alive. The audience wants to feel something emotionally because of the way things are presented.

Why do people get so nervous? Why are they afraid to take on the best chance to show off their knowledge, personality, and ability to connect?

For me, there are three things associated with the nerves.

- **The Unknown** – What will happen? What does my audience expect from me? Will I be able to engage them?
- **Forgetting** – The "mental power outage" as I call it. What if I lose my place, or the flow of the presentation is knocked off course? Or what if you leave out important or key material when your big moment comes?
- **Unanticipated Questions** – Will I be ready for all the questions I might get? People are often frightened by the possibility they might not have the answer to an important question. The loss of credibility in front of an audience is something nobody wants and being embarrassed can lead to never wanting to take the stage again.

I get all of it. And I've been there too.

It wasn't long ago that a man about to take the stage for one of his first really big speaking opportunities said to me, "The anxiety is killing me! I don't think I can calm my nerves."

I could have said a whole bunch of things, but the look on his face told me that not much was going to stick if I rambled on with long-winded, last-minute advice. So, I kept it simple. I'll tell you what I said in a moment.

The fact is, everyone has a degree of anxiety when getting up to speak. Everyone wrestles with finding the best way to combat the internal chaos of nerves, excitement, and energy that goes with making a speech or delivering in front of an audience.

If you don't have nerves, then the talk or presentation probably doesn't mean that much to you and a lack of passion about your subject will be obvious to everyone.

So, what do we need to do?

First and foremost, don't let your mind tell you that you are "nervous." Let your mind tell you that you're anxious. There is a huge difference. Anxious means you're dealing with energy. Nervous means you are scared or uncomfortable about the potential outcome.

The best presenters love competition and see the stage as the scene for a high-stakes payoff. They fear nothing and take aim at everything in front of them.

The key to calming yourself is to make sure you bring a relaxed focus from the very beginning. The fact is, for less experienced public speakers, the opening moments are the most critical and most nerve-wracking.

Here are three things you can do in the early moments of your talk to get off to a positive start. I do each and every one of these – without fail – every time I take the stage.

- **Find a friend and laugh a bit** – Whether you are at a table with others before hitting the stage, mingling with guests in a cocktail hour, or sitting in a conference room before standing before the group, there is the chance to engage and the chance to talk. Sitting alone (or standing) silently makes your mind focus only on the speech and just increases your nervousness. Relax, joke with people, and take your mind off the big moment.

- **Bring quick energy** – Start with a smile, pose a question, show your enthusiasm, and make sure you give them a visual clue that you aren't nervous. Go off script a bit to come across as natural and conversational. Starting off trying to be "perfect" makes you seem rehearsed.
- **Take the focus off you** – A great opening shouldn't take long. Getting to a great video or a key slide or perhaps even going so far as to *walk off the stage* into the audience with a question that makes *someone else* talk can help. Movement often helps relax you. Standing stiffly and facing a big audience can add to your nervousness.

I can't make your nerves go away. It happens for everyone. But, it's really not a bad thing. The key is to embrace the moment and find a way to make any butterflies you may be feeling *fly in unison.*

So, back to the story of the man overcome with stress.

Here is what I said. *"Enjoy the moment. Somebody picked you to do this. Don't be what you think they want you to be -- just be you and make sure you smile and have fun."*

Remember, there is a difference between nerves and anxiety. Standing out when you stand up requires confidence to overcome the very things that might derail others. So, find your way into a mindset that has you anxiously excited to walk in front of your audience, but not afraid of it.

If you want to win with your story, find your own way to a personal calm before you present it. Great things can come from your big moment. Never forget that.

KRAIG'S LIST

3 THINGS: Planning Your Presentation

FIRST 8 SECONDS: Critical first impression sets the tone. Only one shot to win attention.

ONE KEY MESSAGE: What is it? How relevant is will it be to your audience?

HOW I DELIVER: What's my style? How can I involve my audience to keep engagement?

KANN LEADERSHIP

CHAPTER EIGHT

Presentation Skills To Win

Make Them Remember YOU

It's not the size of the room that makes for a great presentation. It's the size of the message. Make it relatable and shareable.

Can you think of the one college professor who blew you away with both the knowledge and intellectual insight that motivated you to think bigger and bolder about the subject you were studying? Who was the person who taught a class you couldn't wait to attend in anticipation of what they might say?

Now ask yourself this; Do you remember the information he or she shared? Or do you remember the person who delivered it and inspired you?

I assume you remembered the speaker and not the information. That is the power of being a great presenter.

Exceptional presenters stick in our memory bank for years and we pull deposits throughout our career from what we remember.

Years later, it's the people we remember and not their information. But there might just be a saying or two, or a quote that was repeated over and over to the point you couldn't help but remember.

I'll share a quote from one such professor who delivered something that has stuck with me for years in just a few pages.

We had a small group each day in our broadcast journalism class – perhaps fifteen to twenty. It wasn't a huge lecture hall. I'm fairly confident that much of what our journalism class carries with us in our careers originated from that very small, quaint classroom.

Years later, this particular professor delivered a specific quote that carries on for me. I use it in almost every presentation I give.

Some of the rooms are small, and some are quite large, with more than five hundred people. My point is that if you are truly delivering a message that has power, it will carry on no matter how many were in the room to receive it. In other words, it's not the size of the room that matters, it's the size of the message being delivered.

If a group of ten or fifteen has two, or even just one person who casts a wide net in professional relationships or social following. In that case, that message suddenly carries a lot of weight and reaches an audience far greater than the size of the room where it originated.

Before you deliver your next talk, deliver yourself to the room where you'll make it. Familiarizing yourself with the environment is paramount.

So how do we make people remember what you want them to remember?

It can't just be about what you say. It has to be about connecting with the audience and making them feel like you are talking to them and not a room full of people.

The great thing about being a presenter is that every speaking opportunity is a chance to connect and create an impression that stays in the head of those who walk out the door long after you're done. And with that, I have one goal every time I speak -- to have fun myself and make sure the audience is right there with me.

People want to connect with a speaker. They really do. They want to relate. They want to see the best of YOU.

So how can you make that impact? How can you present the best version of yourself that delivers a "connection?"

Here are three things that will allow you to deliver your own brand and create an atmosphere that allows people to remember that you were the person standing in front of them.

- **Your personal expertise**—Remember, you were chosen for the stage for a reason. You've done something worthy, been part of company successes, and built a resume along the way that is unique to you. It's yours. Share with people. Let them know your successes and experiences and also your failures. That shows your value and your authenticity.
- **Your personal philosophy**—Everyone has an opinion about something. Learn how to share yours and weave commentary into your conversation with the audience. That stuff is memorable. I'm always interested in people who stand for something or have strong feelings about something, or a vision about how to achieve something. Your vision is yours alone. While others may share your vision, your unique delivery is tied directly to how they receive it.
- **Your personal stories**—Every keynote I do includes audience participation. I start by asking someone who they are and why we should care. Then, I share my story—the kid who grew up only wanting to be a broadcaster, making his own "sports page" and delivering it on my block because I felt the Chicago Tribune and Sun-Times weren't delivering enough

coverage and I wanted to share my own ideas. You know the rest. After I take it to where I am today, I will again challenge those in the audience to answer the question, "Who are YOU, and why should we care?" Most haven't thought about their own value, let alone their personal story, because they don't know if it's "worthy." But everyone has a story. Everyone has stories of their experiences and their journey. Find a way to toss those into your audience's minds because it gives people a chance to know you and why you were chosen to deliver your philosophy and experience.

The CEO of a major global corporation once told me that he didn't really like delivering "keynotes" because he felt like he was "just talking." He said he much preferred a moderator and the ability to answer questions that lead into his company story and personal message. He wanted the interaction of a Q&A because he felt it humanized him and helped to add credibility to his message. He felt he was talking ***with*** people instead of 'to' people.

That leads me to another important thing about being a great presenter who builds a brand in front of an audience. We have to turn the idea of *giving a speech* into delivering a conversation. Talking with your audience, not at them. And we have to think about what they will take away from our conversation.

My full-time television career spanned twenty-five years. That meant roughly two hundred and fifty days a year in the studio. And, conservatively, a minimum of two shows a day. That's 12,500 shows hosted during my television career – at a bare minimum.

Whether it was a studio desk, couch, chair, or podium featured on the set, it was, and I was, a part of a stage. I always knew that once the red light went on, it was time to make something happen. It was a chance to spread the news, share the opinion, or react to the day's event. Simply "getting through it" was never an option.

Something I was taught many years ago has stuck with me throughout my professional career. My hope is that it helps you too.

I was told that "at some point, you'll find yourself on a stage of great importance and you'd better do something with it."

The way I took it was that I'd better focus on the end result possibilities well ***before*** I took that stage.

So, I'll leave you with this. The next time you get the stage and the time, prepare to connect as much as you prepare to convince. Share things that create emotion with your audience. The right mix of personality and authentic style that connects with the audience means people will forever remember that you were the one standing up in front of them.

If you want to win with your story, present a powerful you. And be a "personable you" as well. Personality and style will beat random information every time.

KRAIG'S LIST

3 THINGS: People Want From Their Speaker

EXPERIENCE: An expert who's been there and done that ... differently than others.

A PHILOSOPHY: Someone who stands up, stands out and stands for something.

A CONNECTION: Personal style that attracts and a message that hits home.

KANN LEADERSHIP

MY STORY

The College Years

Having a Purpose and a Game Plan

Did you ever use the Lovejoy's College Guide? It was the most comprehensive reference book for colleges and universities that one could find.

I poured through that massive book day after day for months during my high school career. I was fascinated by the list of schools and the possibilities of where I might land for a college experience. It told you everything you needed to know to narrow your list of prospective schools.

I had a few colleges I was considering. My dad took me on trips to the University of Iowa, Indiana University, and a few smaller schools where I actually considered punting for the football team. My dad went to DePauw University in Greencastle, Indiana, and I had received a letter from their football coach. I also looked at Ohio University because of its radio and television program and a potential chance to try out as a punter.

But in all my research about schools, one thought kept coming back to me. Television.

My dad and I went on a trip to the University of Missouri in Columbia, and I fell in love with the place. Known for its world-renowned journalism school, Missouri was far enough away and close enough to get home. About seven hours from the Chicago suburbs I called home, so many things stood out about Mizzou.

The landmark columns in the central campus area where students congregate became my visual when sorting through college opportunities. I liked the football and basketball that was played in what used to be the Big 8 Conference, and I liked the trees and the architecture on campus. But what stood out was the local NBC affiliate unique to the University.

KOMU-TV was and still is the prime television station in the Columbia-Jefferson City market and Missouri broadcast journalism students served as reporters during their junior and senior years – provided you were admitted to the journalism school with the requisite grades after your sophomore year. At the time, a 3.0 GPA was required for consideration. No easy task. I'm sure it weeded out a lot of talented people who might have had great careers.

Given that I wanted to be a broadcaster, this felt like the right place for me.

Also on campus was the *Columbia Missourian* newspaper and KBIA radio, where journalism students had their chance to produce and deliver news and sports updates and learn the ropes.

Here's a side note.

I found my way into a walk-on tryout for the Missouri Tigers football team as a punter. I wasn't the only one. Among several, we were given about ten punts – against the wind – to show off our leg. Given that you never saw my name in any college box score, media guide, or on any highlight reel, you can imagine how that went.

Did I tell you it was windy that day?

As I like to tell it, I fair caught about two of my own punts blown back to me in the tryout and decided I'd focus on my television career and join a fraternity. I'm joking, but you get the point. And I've exaggerated the story over the years to get a few more laughs.

Here's what I can tell you about fraternity life in those days. Hazing was alive and well and I actually got a lot from it – beyond the ability to do one hundred push-ups at a time - that helped me long term. And the friendships have lasted for years.

I pledged Delta Upsilon. While we weren't the biggest house on campus, we had an amazing group of athletes and "social superstars." Making grades to get into journalism school became quite a challenge in what was then the largest Greek System west of the Mississippi River. Interfraternity sports were a big deal on the Mizzou campus and I loved every bit of playing some very competitive flag football, basketball, and softball. To this day, guys like John Holdsworth, Ron Hauck, Mark Yaeger, and Todd Dietrich have remained among my best friends. And we have years of annual golf trips to back it up.

In all, I lived with about 100 guys at 711 Maryland Avenue in the DU fraternity house. During my junior year, I was the social chairman, which meant coordinating parties with other fraternity houses and sororities. To be honest, the campus was far from dry in those days and I ran the house social budget into a deficit. As my story goes, that's one of the reasons I got elected as president for my senior year. Basically, my fellow brothers bought into my campaign idea that "I made the mess, so now let me fix it."

Thankfully, I had some fellow journalism students in the house. One was Todd Johnson. He was a Texan of the highest order who also had his heart set on a broadcast career. Together, we challenged each other in our opportunities at KOMU and others in the DU house would watch us on television and let us know how bad we were. Holdsworth, my pledge brother, roommate, and great friend, always critiqued the tie choice I made each day and tried to get me to wear his, so he felt some ownership in my "career." He was an agriculture major, which never required wearing makeup for any class projects, unlike my chosen path. My ties were better.

Anchoring at KOMU-TV
Columbia, MO

Our journalism class included some real talents. Kids came from all parts of the United States and beyond to attend the Missouri Journalism School and it wasn't easy to rise above. That proved to be a good thing.

John Anderson – of ESPN *SportsCenter* fame – was one of my mentors. He made it pretty clear that you had to find a way to separate yourself.

I survived a stress-filled try-out to anchor the morning cut-ins at 7:25 and 8:25 during the *"Today Show"* and also found my way into a rotation anchoring the noon news and weekend sports during my junior and senior years.

Like Anderson, guys like Dan Lucy, Brian Neuner, Chris Gervino, and Dave Hunziker left their mark on the sports side. Neuner and Gervino have each stayed in Columbia and worked professionally at the local affiliates covering sports. They've been a big part of hosting Mizzou sports shows, traveling with teams and mentoring students with similar dreams. Gervino is a part of the *Mizzou Sports Network* covering football and basketball as part of the on-air broadcast team – a pretty cool dream job if you love the Tigers. Hunziker left town and has been the voice of the Oklahoma State Cowboys for years.

We had very talented news reporters and anchors who've had stellar careers. Steve Daniels would be one. He left Mizzou and started his career in Tucson as his first job, which is pretty hard to do. Soon after, he was off to Denver and then found his way to a role on *Dateline NBC*. We had producers who wound up in top-ten markets pretty quickly and I must not forget Angie Krauss, who vaulted up the career ladder and landed as a producer on Oprah Winfrey's show.

I think we all looked up to each other for our individual talents. We all had the passion. We all understood that the road wasn't going to be easy. Among many things, being a part of the Missouri School of Journalism taught us that competition was the norm and we'd better get used to it.

Like everyone who worked as a student at KOMU, I learned how to tell a visual story. We shot our own video, edited our own stories, and made them ready for air. We were blessed with great mentors and instructors who truly invested their time in making each of us a valuable part of "The Mizzou Mafia" – the legacy of reporters, anchors, videographers, producers, directors, and even news directors who'd gone on to have long professional careers in broadcast journalism. We have stayed in touch, helped each other land jobs, critiqued each other's work, and have always promoted the brand that is *Mizzou*.

Speaking of brands, that's where I learned that if I didn't build my own, I'd never make it.

There were simply too many students who all wanted the same success in the same business, sending tapes to the same list of news directors. Chances were almost one hundred percent that if you'd sent your tape to the station in Yakima, Washington or Yuma, Arizona, three or four others had done the same thing. Want to be a sports anchor in Montgomery, Alabama, or Macon,

Georgia, to get your start? There were two or three in my class who wanted the same job.

Stacey Woelfel and Kent Collins were instructors in the journalism school and a big part of the day-to-day operation at KOMU. Woelfel had been at WESH-TV in Orlando and brought great experience to us. Collins is a legend in the eyes of many and I'll share more on Kent's influence on me later in the book. John Quarderer was another with a big impact on all of us. I remember a million things they told us during our shifts at the station or while in their classroom. But one thing has always stood out.

Here's the quote I was referring to a few pages back. Kent Collins was one of the faculty members who taught us in those small classrooms.

Collins, now a member of the journalism school's hall of fame, said, "You can't preach to anyone unless you get them into the church."

His message was profound. His point was that nobody would watch your story on the news in full unless the first fifteen seconds were compelling enough to get them to pay attention and lock in.

I never forgot it and to this day, I use it in every seminar or keynote I deliver. To me, it applies in every walk of life. If we want people to take notice of us or what we do, then we'd better give people a reason to come pay attention. Reeling people in is the toughest challenge. Once we get them there, we have to over-deliver on their expectations. That's how brands are built.

My resume tape upon leaving KOMU and the University of Missouri might not have been the best in the country from a twenty-two-year-old graduate looking for a first job in the business, but I learned that it had to showcase the best of ***me.***

I had spent four years going to class, knowing full well my career of choice would require me to be different and talented. I soaked up every bit of experience there was – be it academically, socially with my fraternity leadership opportunities, in clubs like the Homecoming Steering Committee, and any shift I could get at the television and radio stations. I was constantly on the go.

When I speak on any college campus, my advice to students is that they'd better find a way to separate themselves from the rest. In small classes or big lecture halls, they sit next to people they are comfortable with, not realizing that the very person to their left or right is most likely a competitor looking for the same job upon graduation.

What makes you different? What makes you special? Brands begin long before we're established in our careers. They begin early and my college days at Missouri were one reminder after another that I'd better be ready to be a cut above.

My journey into the professional ranks and navigating the path to a dream landing spot was about to begin.

CHAPTER NINE
Media Opportunities to Win

A Message that Belongs to YOU

Before you think about chasing the media for exposure, first figure out what you want to say. What's your message? It all begins with that.

Do you want to build a brand that gets attention? Find your way into the media and then make the most of it.

I grew up wanting to be a sportscaster. For many of my early years, it's all I thought about. If I made my way to reaching that goal, which would mean a career in media and a big part of that would be a role interviewing athletes, coaches, and other leaders in the sports industry.

No problem! It couldn't come fast enough.

It was something I practiced in my head and rehearsed in my mind long before I ever got the chance to do it for a living. Over the years, in the childhood bedroom I described, calling make-believe games, I would also play out the interviews with the athletes from those games.

"Big win tonight by the Bears," I would say. "And I'm here now with the great Walter Payton who rushed for 176 yards and scored three touchdowns in today's win over the Green Bay Packers."

On went the interview with various questions, I would ask. Standing in for Walter Payton would be whatever friend was lucky enough to be over to my house that day. Actually, they kind of enjoyed it.

As I evolved professionally, I was pointing a microphone in the direction of city leaders, corporate executives, politicians, and athletes and coaches from all sports. I've always loved the interaction and the challenge of creating an atmosphere that allowed for fun banter and conversation interesting for the audience. I felt like if I could get them to say something of interest, and get them to deliver it with a smile and maybe a few laughs, I would have "won the session."

My point in sharing is to show that I have a passion for interviewing others. I always have. And I'm not alone. I would venture to say that every journalist started off to do fair journalism and have meaningful and respectful relationships with the subjects they cover.

Being on the other side and hoping for fair and honest coverage requires looking at the media as an opportunity to share your story or information.

Obviously, not every interview is fun and games. Dignitaries or city leaders have agendas and speaking points they're bound and determined to put out there regardless of the questions that come their way. Coaches speak in "coach speak," making sure not to give away too much information or too much confidence. Some interviews can become confrontational when there is tension about the subject or a fractured relationship between the person being interviewed and the media outlet pointing the camera or holding the tape recorder.

It's a game. And "winning the media interview" means understanding the subject you're talking to and the subject matter you're discussing. It means establishing a "safe zone" for the interview, where everyone feels relaxed and comfortable. It also means asking questions you believe the audience wants asked while making sure you tell the story in the process.

Both the interviewer and the interview subject have brands at stake. A good interview does wonders for the media reporter's credibility and brand. At the same time, the person on the other end must realize that whatever is said, and how it is said, determines how they'll be viewed as well as how their team, organization or company will be viewed.

For those ready to be interviewed, I always emphasize preparation. Without thinking before the record button is hit about what might occur or what you want to get across, you've basically thrown away the chance to make a bigger, smarter impact on your audience.

Why are interviews and sharing your personal story so important to the media? For the same reason Reality TV is so popular. People like transparency, authenticity, and a feeling of connection. But you have to let them in.

Ask yourself, "Do I wing it, or do I work it?"

More importantly, you'd better have *a message.*

Trust me when I say that everyone who is good to great on the receiving end of questions has a real message. With that overall message comes things they MUST say if they are to succeed with their opportunity.

As someone who has been fortunate to have interviewed superstar athletes, celebrities and presidents, I know when someone is there merely to be interviewed, or there to intentionally and artfully *deliver a message*. There's a huge difference. Again, it's opportunity over obligation.

Remembering your brand and reputation is at stake, here are my three pieces of advice the next time you are given an interview platform:

- **Know your information and know the interviewer**—The first part is obvious and the second gives you an idea of what you are in for. Will you be drilled with questions, or will you be engaged in conversation? Those are two very different approaches because a conversationalist provides a sense of dialogue over a sound bite.
- **Know your message**—This is the most important thing. Going into an interview without a real "message" is a waste of time. You've given up all control and are simply filling in someone else's blanks.
- **Have a "three things list"**—I advise this of everyone. While preparing and working on your message, identify the three things you need your audience to know *regardless of the questions!* Ask yourself, "What do I need them to leave with?" or "What must they know about me and my values?" or "What do I want them to share with others?"

The easiest way to gain confidence going into an interview is to have the answer to *WHY? Why am I here?* If you don't have the answer to that, then you don't have a purpose. All you have is an unused platform.

And for those looking to take their career and their brand to the next level, making sure you understand the value in the opportunity is the first step to something a whole lot bigger for you.

If you want to win with your story, see the big picture when it comes to the media.

KRAIG'S LIST

3 THINGS: To Understand About The Media

HERE AND GROWING: Fact of life and much needed watchdog and checks and balances.

SHAPES AND PRESENTS: A powerful storyteller that can greatly affect image and brand.

ALWAYS, ALWAYS: Gets the final say and the last word... period.

KANN
LEADERSHIP

CHAPTER TEN

Media Opportunities to Win

Find a Way To Make Them Notice YOU

Want to get noticed by the media? Be better or uniquely different at what you do than others and make sure you have a message worth selling. They'll find you.

If we're looking to advance our brand, we have to make our brand stand out. The media can help present it to the masses. But again, we have to realize the gift of the media *opportunity*.

During my time at the LPGA, I had an athlete's agent question me one time about why their client hadn't been chosen to take part among chosen athletes for a big marketing campaign in the works. My answer to the agent was very straight forward.

"Take a minute for me and ask yourself what your athlete did with the last big opportunity they were presented?"

In a phone call, the agent shared the client's lengthy resume as a way of saying I had missed something in my decision. No question, it was impressive. But I wasn't buying it.

To me, media opportunities are earned. The athlete in question had turned down a huge opportunity a few weeks prior to represent the organization – and themself – at a global press conference that would reach media outlets in numerous countries. Four athletes were asked, three gladly participated when asked. My team had to find a fourth after the athlete in question took a pass. To me, it was a huge opportunity for the athlete to promote themselves and also represent their sponsors.

Understandably, athletes themselves have questioned me about why they weren't included in big platform media events and why others are hand-picked more often.

It's really pretty simple.

Some got excited beyond words about the chance to represent the organization. Others seemed to find excuses about why the timing wasn't just right or quickly explained that there was a burden attached to readjusting their schedule.

On one occasion, an athlete looked a bit confused by my decision to go in another direction, but then realized that she hadn't taken the last opportunity very seriously.

She hadn't put forth her best effort to represent the organization, the event being discussed, or herself. And in doing so, she had created a feeling in me that it didn't mean very much to be included, which led me down a different path - away from her - when I had a need.

Interviews aren't just about questions and answers.

They are about enthusiasm, first and foremost.

They are about body language and the environment that's created as the interview plays out. They are about thinking well in advance about what might be asked or what might need to be said.

The questions are important for sure. But they are just a jumping-off point, or a means of delivering the messages you shape in advance.

And then there is the frustration from some that the media just doesn't seem too interested in providing coverage.

I've heard it from athletes and executives, agents and even public relations specialists; "Why aren't media folks paying attention or interested in my story?"

That's a complex question, for sure. And it usually has many layers. But the fundamental issue centers on how compelling your story is and how well you are able to deliver it.

Think about how many interviews you've heard and then consider how much you remember from watching and listening to the person being interviewed. Ask yourself:

- Did the person have a real message?
- Did the person share a compelling story?
- Did the person challenge the question with a strong opinion or stance?

Often times, those who get the opportunity to answer questions or sit on a panel discussion simply just answer the questions. There is no passion behind the comments, no thought behind the opinion, and frequently no real opinion at all.

Media folks are looking for quotes and they're looking for value statements or opinion. It's as simple as that.

Media interviews aren't about just answering the questions that come your way. They're about shaping messages in advance that you deliver thanks to their questions.

Those in TV are hunting for a 30-second news clip with some real staying power. They will want to re-play it over and over again as commentary material for their on-air analysts or anchors.

Print media folks are looking for the juicy comment that can create a headline and draw both readers and page views. That's their reality.

As the subject of an interview, you may be saying, "Well, why would I really want that?" or "Who really needs to be the subject of everyone's attention?"

I'll spin it this way. Do you want people to know your story? Do you want more attention for your brand? Do you want to be relevant?

Most people do.

In today's media world, a big way to be notable is to *be quotable*. So, when you've got a date with the microphone and a reporter or interviewer seated across from you, anticipate the questions and think about what you might say. In the same way that speechwriters take time to craft the right words for the right impact, think about what you want people to remember. Then deliver it with enough energy and confidence to make it happen.

Audiences want to be given something they can hold onto.

Other things to consider:

- **The media is unforgiving of a slip-up or a misspeak**—Especially if it's a situation – sports or business – that carries with it a great deal of attention. Some moments are bigger than others, and when they're big, the media hangs on your every word. When they aren't big, the media can turn something small into something big in a real hurry.
- **Think before you speak**—What's the worst thing about taking a few moments after a game or practice before you visit with media? Nothing. So, just do it. Same goes for the time prior to a big press conference announcing your corporate news. You spend a lot of time on your craft, your announcement, your sport, or your business, so why not spend a few extra minutes to make sure you explain yourself correctly when it matters most.
- **The follow up is magnified more than ever**—We live in a world of analysis, debate, conjecture, and speculation. Nobody is immune to the media microscope. It's important to gather your thoughts, be on point, and make sure you're not soon working on a retraction or clarification.

Your brand hinges on what you say and how others present what you say.

Lastly, when questions are coming at you and one stands out that could be the defining moment of the interview, pause is a powerful thing.

There is nothing wrong with giving a question some thought as opposed to just talking away and working your way toward an

A Fun Media Moment with Major Champion Stacy Lewis

answer somewhere in there. Being "over-coached" before jumping into a media circus isn't a good thing as it makes people seem rehearsed and hurts the all-important transparency that creates trust and connection. Taking a few minutes to seem prepared is something I'll always push for. In one simple word… take time to *anticipate.*

When it comes to getting people to pay attention, the media is a valuable target to go after. If they pay attention and take the time to share your story or the story of your organization, your audience size immediately goes up. There is greater awareness of your product and also your people. Media becomes a major voice.

Opportunities don't come along for everyone. You have to work for it. And the reach of your story is largely dependent on how you are able to present it. Present it well and you elevate your brand creating a longer lifespan of media attention. Present it poorly and the window of time for media coverage shrinks. Fewer people will hear about you and the size of your group of followers is diminished.

The bottom-line result is greatly influenced by how you use the stage you are given. When the media presents you with an opportunity to tell your story, you'd better be ready because the media is listening closely.

If you want to win with your story, consider how the media will react to the way you deliver it. You'll be glad you did. So will your brand.

KRAIG'S LIST

3 THINGS: About Your Big Media Interview

HAVE CONTROL: Of yourself first. Calmness wins. Smile before you start.

RESPONSE IS KING: Power is in the direction of the answer not the question. Prepare.

RESPECT IS BIG: Respect the interviewer and the opportunity you have to deliver.

KANN LEADERSHIP

MY STORY

Chasing My First Job

The Winding Path to a Network Landing Spot

I have saved every rejection letter I ever received along the way to my first opportunity.

While some might have tossed them in the trash, shredded them in disgust, or turned them into paper airplanes, I found a useful purpose.

For me, it served as motivation and a nice paper trail of proof that landing a job in television was no small task. We've all been rejected at some point. Finding a way to see the positive in it should become our first goal before moving on.

I still laugh at the first job offer I ever received. It was a small station in Greenville, North Carolina, and the offer on the table was a whopping $10,050.00 per year to be a news reporter. After visiting the station and receiving the offer, I was ticked. And, admittedly a bit overconfident about my worth. I made a mistake. It was a lesson that served me well for years to come.

In short, I sent a letter to the station's news director telling him that I felt I was worth more and had been insulted by his offer. The trouble was that I sent the letter on KOMU stationary and not my own personal letterhead.

Quickly, news of my letter circled back to John Quarderer, my news director at KOMU. John was a no-nonsense news director and a man I respected greatly. He wasn't happy about having one of his students fire off a letter to a fellow news director telling him what he could do with his opportunity. Rightly so.

As a small consolation, John said my letter was actually well written, made a strong point, and spoke positively about my classmates' merits about the skillset we had to offer news directors upon graduation. I guess my print journalism class hadn't been a waste of time after all!

John's main issue was my use of the station's stationary and that I had popped off to a news director. Neither was in my best interest – nor the best interest of John himself, who would hope to see a few of his students land their first job in Greenville at some point. It hurt my brand and wasn't great for John's, either. It also wasn't great for the rest of my classmates.

I got the message. It helped me understand that turning down a job is one thing, but turning someone off in the process can hurt your reputation long-term. John doesn't know it, but that experience was huge for me.

For the record, I did ask the news director in Greenville if he meant $10,500.00 and not $10,050.00. He didn't.

I graduated from Mizzou in May of 1988. Greenville wasn't the only job I'd been offered that didn't seem like the right fit and I didn't accept an offer until November.

During those five months, I stayed on campus, biding my time and making as much money as I could to pay for an apartment and cover the costs of shipping resumes and resume tapes. I also used the time to give back to younger students with the same dream.

I also kept my other job at *Southside Liquors*, the local shop for all things a college student should have in moderation.

The job at *Southside Liquors* provided me some tutoring about customer relations, the responsibility of earning a small wage - $4.50 per hour – and another quote that I never forgot.

Southside, as we called it, was owned and run by a husband and wife team, each in their sixties. Marty was the man in charge, but his wife, Rusty, was the one who came in each day to handle the books and make sure guys like me were on the straight and narrow. She watched me on KOMU and always had a few comments for me. Some were quite helpful.

"Kraig," she said. "You need to smile more! If you're not smiling, we're not smiling."

To this day, I think about that and I've shared that in media coaching opportunities and in mentoring young broadcast students as part of the *Dan Patrick School of Sportscasting* at Full Sail University in Orlando.

It really applies to everything we do. If you aren't having fun, then who else is having fun? I think about it when delivering a keynote or during my presentation skills workshops. We need to show people that we like what we're doing.

By the time late fall had rolled around in 1988, I was getting some nibbles from other news directors. While many of my fellow students were busy sending tapes and hoping for the right interview to come their way, I took a different approach.

I reached out to various stations in places that I thought I might like to work, sending my tape, but asking if I could come to see them and get a few minutes of their time. Whether they had a job at the time was irrelevant.

My grandparents lived in Peachtree City, Georgia, just outside Atlanta. Working somewhere in Georgia had been on my mind and I had a plan.

Bill and Margaret Harvey were the most amazing people. They lived many years in suburban Chicago, about a fifteen-minute walk from my house in Western Springs, and I spent a lot of time with them. They came to my games, they took me, my brother Brian and my mom on trips and we're seemingly there for anything that mattered.

My grandfather was the first to introduce me to the game of golf and when they moved to suburban Atlanta, he joined a country club that gave him access to three courses. I made a trip there every summer during my high school years. My grandfather and I played a lot of golf. He loved the early tee times, which wasn't great for a teenager's mission to sleep as long as humanly possible, but it did give me a chance to develop some skills on the course. I still have many of our scorecards.

Georgia had a few small television media markets that grabbed my interest as a potential place to get my start. Albany, Macon, and Columbus were a few of the small cities that I targeted.

Columbus was just a couple of hours from Peachtree City, and I landed an interview with Dick Byrd. He was the news director at WTVM-TV, the ABC affiliate in Columbus. We hit it off and before I knew it, he'd offered me a job as a do-it-all reporter, videographer, and editor. No anchoring opportunities were offered, but the best part was the chance to be a part-time reporter in the sports department. I took the job for a salary of $13,500 per year, which wasn't much but felt like a huge raise over the opportunity to move to Greenville, North Carolina, for $10,050.

Spring Training for WTVM-TV Columbus, GA

And I can tell you that I was more than respectful of Mr. Byrd and the opportunity he was offering.

The longtime news anchor was Dick McMichael and he treated me well. His studio desk partner was Dee Armstrong. She was fantastic to work with. We had a weatherman named Chuck Leonard who made me laugh every day and I learned from every reporter and videographer on staff. The best opportunity came from my work with two sports guys who became my first "mentors" and gave my sports broadcasting career the jump start I needed.

By the way, Columbus was also an early stop for ESPN's Rece Davis, who cut his teeth at the CBS affiliate in town during my tenure at WTVM.

Dave Platta was the lead sports guy at WTVM and Bruce Snyder was his weekend sidekick. I went everywhere with those guys – including a trip with Platta to Spring Training to cover the Houston Astros and Atlanta Braves. Columbus was the minor league home of the *Columbus Mudcats*, which, at the time, was the Double-A affiliate for the Astros. Guys like Scott Servais, Eric Anthony, and Ken Caminiti made their way through Columbus in the Astros farm system.

Snyder took me to cover Auburn football and basketball, which was about a forty-five-minute drive and we also made our way to Atlanta Falcons training camp. I was in heaven and suddenly, my updated resume tape had enough sports to allow for a transition out of news and into sports full-time.

Climbing the ranks in local television means learning, improving, and moving.

I only stayed in Columbus for a year before I was offered my first real sports position.

This time it was Fort Myers, Florida, at WINK-TV, where I was offered the number three sports reporter position in a three-person department. The starting salary was $14,500.00, which wasn't a huge raise but a raise nonetheless and I did get the opportunity for overtime pay, which was a bonus because I knew I'd be working a lot.

John Emmert was the news director and he was a great one. John had lots of experience, and I did a lot more listening than I did talking for one of the first times in my life. He was that good.

My sports cohorts were Kenn Tomasch and Tom Tidey. Tomasch was smooth and he was a really good writer and a very hard worker. Tidey became a good friend while we were together. I was their videographer, but I did my own reports for their sportscasts and anchored them as a fill-in when they needed a day off.

Believe it or not, my co-anchor was Hoda Kotb, now of *Today Show* fame. She was, and is, as good as they come. She's a better person than she even appears on the camera.

There was some talent in that market for sure. Shephard Smith was at the NBC affiliate and climbed the ranks to FOX News Channel. Every sports anchor in the market looked out for one another. At least it felt that way. And that was the beauty of the business back then. Mike Cannington was the lead sports anchor at the ABC affiliate, WEVU-TV, and John Curtis was his weekend sports partner. John Hammes and Jay Severson manned the sports desk at the NBC station, WBBH-TV.

Collectively, we covered the same events, which ranged from Miami Hurricanes, Florida Gators and Florida State Seminoles games on Saturdays, to Miami Dolphins and Tampa Bay Buccaneers football games on Sundays, to Spring Training games and even the Fort Myers Sun Sox of the old Senior Professional Baseball League. Friday night high school football was huge.

With Kenn Tomasch at Super Bowl XXV for WINK-TV Ft. Myers, FL

My highlight might have been the opportunity to cover Super Bowl XXV in Tampa during the Gulf War. I was in heaven. The New York Giants and the Buffalo Bills. Seriously?!

With so much media covering the game and not enough seats for everyone, somehow, I found myself walking around the stadium for the entire fourth quarter, including the moment when Scott Norwood missed the field goal for the Bills. I then ventured into the locker room to shoot the press conference with Bill Parcells and his victorious players afterward. It was a memory for sure.

In our shop, we felt like we had the best sports team. But you know what? It didn't matter. As a band of merry sportscasters from all the stations, we played golf together, played in charity basketball events together, and hung out together.

The best thing that came from my almost three years in Southwest Florida was the opportunity to cover golf. The local PGA TOUR pro was Nolan Henke and he worked with an instructor named Mike Calbot out at Pelican's Next in Bonita Bay.

Each week, I'd head to Calbot's range to shoot his instructional tips that we aired on *WINK-TV*. He called himself "The Golf Doctor" and it was my job to produce, shoot and edit his quick hit lessons for our news shows. Along the way, I met Henke and between the two of them, my passion for golf took off. Not only did I get some free lessons, but I also made a couple of friendships that remain to this day.

As Henke was winning his three tournaments on the PGA TOUR, I felt like I was along for the ride. Years later, when I reached The Golf Channel and was serving as a PGA TOUR beat reporter, he was still on the circuit and having success. It brought things full circle.

Naples, Florida has had a long-standing tie to the PGA TOUR's senior circuit and during my time at WINK, the PGA TOUR Champions tournament brought the likes of Arnold Palmer, Lee Trevino and Chi Chi Rodriguez to town. I had my chances to report and interview some of the biggest names in the game. A few years later, that came in real handy.

A couple of professional stories stand out for me during my time in Fort Myers. And a personal one too.

I'll never forget my first chance to anchor the weekend sports at *WINK*. The six o'clock newscast meant coming in around one o'clock, preparing your rundown and writing your scripts while recording the big sports events of the day. As events would finish, you'd begin editing your highlights for the sportscast.

Eager for my first day on the set, I drove into the station about eleven in the morning and began to write. In writing your sportscast, you wrote an "on-camera intro," which was supposed to be fairly short – perhaps ten seconds. The intro carried into the highlights which carried into the scoreboard graphic and then onto the next on-camera or perhaps straight to another highlight.

For whatever reason, I felt the need to set up the highlights and my "intros" became books! When the moment of truth came on the air, I barely got through half of my sportscast before running out of my allotted time. It's not that I made mistakes, I just misjudged the time as though I'd never done a sportscast in my life. It was a huge learning experience that day and I'm sure my more seasoned co-anchor, Jane Lorenzini, knew exactly what had happened.

I never forgot it, and from that day on, it was short intros and a fast-paced sportscast with more video and less Kraig Kann. At least I smiled. And I'm sure that would have made my old boss at *Southside Liquors* proud.

My second memory was both personal and professional, all wrapped into one wild week.

About a year into my two-and-a-half-year tenure in Fort Myers, I proposed to my girlfriend, Kim Powers.

She, too, went to Mizzou, which is where we met. I had some fun asking her for an ID at *Southside Liquors* despite knowing she was twenty-one. Clearly, it was my way of getting in good with the sorority girl I'd had my eye on. And one of her sorority sisters was one of the sharper students in my broadcast class. Jill Bauer went on to a career with *QVC*, where she was a recognizable mainstay for years. She played a role in our relationship because she told each of us that we might be a good match. We dated all of our senior year and Kim was as understanding and supportive as one could be for a guy who was about to chase a television career.

I left for Columbus in November, and she graduated from Mizzou that December. She took the risk to join my crazy life in Columbus and moved there soon after graduation. Six months later, I received the offer to go to Fort Myers to do sports full-time and she stayed back to serve out the terms of her apartment lease - a huge commitment. Once that was done, she moved again to be with me in Fort Myers, and after about a year, I realized I'd better wise up and propose or risk losing her. She said, "Yes."

About a year later, in February of 1991, I received a call from WWMT-TV in Kalamazoo, Michigan, about an opening for a weekend sportscaster. This was my chance! A regular anchor spot and a big role in the thirty-sixth market in the country. Kalamazoo by itself isn't big, but when you add Grand Rapids and Battle Creek, the tri-cities make for a nice audience. I had sent my tape. They clearly liked what they saw and wanted to bring me up for an interview.

But there was a slight problem. We were scheduled to be married in St. Louis on March 2nd – only a week later. I never told anyone at WINK-TV about the opportunity to interview because you just don't do that. They wanted me in Kalamazoo for an interview the week of our wedding. Clearly, there was a conflict.

"What are you doing on Friday, March 1?" asked news director Mike Rindo.

Hah! Not much, just attending my rehearsal dinner was my answer.

As it all worked out, we flew to St. Louis early in the week. I flew to Kalamazoo and WWMT-TV on a Wednesday morning, interviewed, and flew back Wednesday night. And would you believe I was so overwhelmed with the week's events that I never asked when they'd be making a decision?

Somehow, they tracked me down and offered me the job Friday morning. A whopping base salary of $25,000 per year. I was thrilled and without hesitation, I took it without even negotiating for more. I didn't have the time or the energy. I was ready to be a sports anchor with a regular slot and I couldn't have been more excited. That night at the rehearsal dinner for our wedding, we announced that we would be moving to Michigan soon after the honeymoon.

Just how crazy is the business of television?

Upon arriving home from our week-long honeymoon trip to Jamaica, there was a message on our answering machine from Kenn Tomasch, the sports director at my station in Fort Myers. "Hey, short-timer," he said. "We hear you are leaving for a new opportunity. Look forward to seeing you when you get back to work."

Wait, what?

I hadn't told a single person about my interview. Not one.

But here's how the business works. Somebody else who was in the running for the job in Kalamazoo had called the station for an update and was told they'd hired someone. Their follow up question was, "Where are they coming from?" Clearly, their first call was to WINK in Fort Myers to say that they heard there was an opening in the sports department. When Tomasch and Tidey probably looked at each other and neither had a new job to report, it was easy to figure out that I was leaving. News breaks fast in the television world.

Kalamazoo became the launching pad for me. I worked with John Koch. He was the sports director, a California native who'd been in Nebraska prior to Michigan. He was a guy with a very fixed routine and a unique style. We got along well and made a nice splash in the market – especially with high school sports.

Two things stood out during our pairing together. First, was our *"Channel 3 High School Top Twenty"* – a weekly poll during the football and basketball season. We went across West Michigan doing a team feature a night leading up to the season and counted down to Channel 3's number one team. Our poll came out fresh every Monday night and people started following it.

Who cared about the statewide rankings! To us, the only poll that mattered was ours!

At season's end, we had an awards event on-site at a hotel during our "Sports Extra" segment. Pretty cool for the kids and their school. At least we thought so.

What else were we known for? Golf!

Koch and I got in our fair share of rounds throughout West Michigan. And then came the idea for ranking the best eighteen public golf holes in the entire region. We called it the "Koch & Kann Fantasy 18." A mix of par fours, fives, and threes adding up to a par 72 layout. With some fun brainstorming sessions, we had it turned into a scorecard that we had sponsored and delivered to courses that had the honor of having one of our featured holes. Not a bad marketing plan. And it got better.

As we featured one hole per week for eighteen weeks, we felt we had to have a payoff. And that was the concept of playing all eighteen holes – in ONE day. And that's what we did during the summer of 1994.

Solstice is the longest day of the year each June, and we rented a limo and began at 4:00 a.m. that morning driving out to Benton Harbor to tee off. Each of the eighteen courses would be visited, with live shots for our newscasts throughout the day and culminating that night with a live remote from the final course on our trail at eleven o'clock. To play all eighteen holes, you had to play quick! We got it done. An amazing feat that drew a lot of attention in the area. As I remember it, the sprinklers went off behind us – and on us – during our nighttime eleven o'clock news live shot. Fitting, I guess.

I'm grateful for so much in my career. WWMT was a blessing. It was my biggest chance yet to grow and find myself as an anchor and I worked with some amazing people who are friends to this day. Barry Shanley and Judy Markee were the main news anchors during the week. A great duo – Shanley was a real character and loved to hear himself talk. He joked about it, made shows fun and he was very passionate about the community. Jim Mertens was my news anchor on the weekends and we had a solid weather team in John Wendell, Keith Thompson, and Peter Chan. Koch and I gave them grief constantly for taking time away from our sportscasts due to "breaking weather." It's a common gripe among sportscasters who take pride in our three minutes of airtime and hate losing it to "lake effect snow" or the "potential for sleet or hail."

Jamie Boll eventually took Shanley's place at the station as Barry transitioned into retirement. Dennis House was another real talent who left for Hartford and has been a mainstay anchor in the Northeast since the early 1990s.

Learning the ropes in local television, you're never too far from your next mistake. I always remember rushing to the set for the eleven o'clock sportscast, sitting down quickly and forgetting to put my microphone on. I remember a few live shots that didn't happen as we lost signal moments before hitting air. And I remember doing a live shot showing highlights of a hockey game without a monitor and having the producer tell me "goal" every time the puck went in the net. It was my job to make it seem as though I saw it all without actually seeing anything. You learn to ad-lib and you learn to learn – if that makes any sense.

Cameramen like Steve Hayes, John Shortt, Chris Kettlewell, Pat Martin, Bill Krupka, Russ Kusler, and Anthony Mobley worked hard to make you look good and I always realized that the more you appreciated their work, the better they'd work to make you look good. We spent long days together and made many trips to cover the Detroit Lions during the Barry Sanders era, the Tigers during the Cecil Fielder era and home games for Michigan, Michigan State, and Notre Dame football.

Western Michigan was our hometown team and we covered them like a glove.

Koch and I traveled with the football and basketball Broncos and televised some of the games as well. Coach Al Molde was a fan of ours and gave us everything we needed from the football team. Bob Donewald was the hoops coach. He was a tougher man than Molde and had a soft side and a real stern side. That was great because it taught us how to handle a coach who ran a tight ship.

I hung out with a local radio sports jock named Scott Melvin. He went by "Scotty Bud," which I thought was pretty good. He was "Bud" to a lot of folks in town and Melvin, Koch, and I were regulars at the Kalamazoo Wings hockey games. The K-Wings were a big deal in town - then the main minor league affiliate for the Dallas Stars. Hall of Fame NHL coach Ken Hitchcock manned the bench at that time and Mike Miller was the "Voice of the K-Wings" before leaving to become the radio play-by-play man for the New Jersey Devils. I learned a lot from Mike and the opportunity to cover hockey. To this day, I don't know what was better, the games or the weekly media lunch at *Damon's The Place for Ribs.*

I could go on and on about the memories in Kalamazoo. It was a special place for me. We bought our first house there and then three months later, life changed again. Big time.

The WWMT-TV News Team: With John Koch, Cindy Dole, Barry Shanley, Keith Thompson, Judy Markee, Jamie Boll, John Wendell

CHAPTER ELEVEN

Media Relationships To Win

Relationships Build Brands for YOU

It's called media relations. Start with that and know that getting the results you want begins with the foundation of strong relationships.

I'll say it again, if you are looking for a great way to get your message or story told, or seeking a way to build brand awareness, the media is a pretty valuable place to start.

But success with the media doesn't come easily. So, let's talk about the relationships you'll need to create media success.

I have always wondered how many people who make their living in marketing communications and crave for and rely upon good press, really know or understand the goals and needs of the media they're chasing. Feeling like you know is one thing. Truly *knowing* is another.

Working to be good *with* the press is important. That's based on an understanding of how to deliver a message.

Working to be good *to* the press is just as important. Many don't see it. They look at media as the enemy or a necessary (or unnecessary) evil and it's unfortunate.

They expect that media will come their way and just deal with it when it happens.

Everyone wants great press, yet when media tells a different story than the story you're hoping for, the fireworks begin. In other words, it's one thing to want good media coverage. Getting it is a work of art. And it's important to know how to get it.

During my time as Chief Communications Officer for the LPGA, we conducted multiple seminars designed to provide our players with a better understanding of media, how it operates, what it's looking for, and how to make use of every opportunity (notice I didn't say obligation) for personal and league brand awareness and brand building.

My goal was to raise the level of interest in our players and, in doing so, raise the awareness of the organization. To me, it began with the athletes.

A big part of the time was spent on the importance of social media as a tool and a lot of it was spent on keys to making the most of an interview. Today, I think they go hand in hand. That interview process begins well before the reporter and the microphone show up. And what gets said in a media setting is quickly pushed to the public via social media. So, it's important – more so than ever – to have a real plan and a clear strategy.

But here is the most important thing;

Knowing positive press is more important than ever, knowing how to treat those who carry the pen, the microphone or the camera is a critical link to success.

Media coverage isn't a given. They have choices. Make sure your news is worthy of attention and then make sure you treat the media with respect for taking the time to cover it.

At the LPGA, we needed as much coverage as we could earn. With that, our communications office focused a lot of time and energy discussing how we would treat those on the other end.

We wanted our story told and we had a strategy to accomplish our goal.

The first thing we did was change our media guide into more of a "player guide" filled with bios and feature information rather than pages and pages of statistical data. Numbers and stats would be outdated before the season was halfway over, while tidbits about the athletes would serve as feature opportunities that we could pitch at a moment's notice.

A Fun Media Moment with Major Champion Brittany Lincicome

We also settled on the idea of a "beat system," not unsimilar to an assignment desk at a city newspaper where someone is in charge of staying connected with the fire department, police, hospitals, city government and other segments that create or serve as hubs for news.

In our case, we focused on golf networks like Golf Channel, golf periodicals like *Golfweek*, *Global Golf Post* and other regionally based golf organizations.

More importantly, we paid great service to media outlets not directly involved with the game where there was a decision to make about what sports were featured and what athletes were highlighted during a given day, week or month. For example; big outlets like the *Wall Street Journal*, or the *New York Times.*

Greater attention was paid to wider scale sports outlets like ESPN, *Sports Illustrated, USA Today* or *Sports Business Journal.*

We wanted great relationships with their writers and editors so they would have our organization more top of mind and consider giving us a segment within their content space.

We also went outside sports. For example, our people created stronger relationships with decision makers at *People* who might consider our athletes worthy of attention as more than just golfers. There were other media avenues to solicit but you get the point.

My philosophy is that before any outlet gives you the coverage, it all goes back to building relationships before the ask is ever made for a spot in their precious real estate.

Believe it or not, media appreciates being cared about when there is actually nothing to cover. They appreciate time with athletes and coaches when there isn't a game on the schedule. They appreciate ideas being tossed their way when they aren't looking.

So, when it comes to building your brand. Consider the media as a great source for more attention. Figure out where you want your story told. Break it down by segments of audience you'd like as consumers, then work on relationships with the media that can deliver your product to those consumers. If you generate enough *attraction* to the brand, you'll gain more *traction* in the marketplace. It all leads to a bigger brand.

My advice is simple; don't be afraid to push your story out there. Just make sure you think about how it's being delivered to them. Then, think about giving media something far greater than they expected when they agreed or chose to come cover your event or game in the first place. Give them bigger access and more unique opportunities to do something they wouldn't normally get to do. It's my belief that being progressive in your thinking and your access opportunities will yield greater coverage when it matters most.

Above all, stress the importance of "relations" ... as in *Media* ***Relations.*** Today's media have different choices and different ways to cover you or your team. They don't have to be there in person to write about it.

Those who succeed are those who can get media to make an appearance and then make it their mission to treat them so well in the process that they can't wait to come back for more.

If you want to win with your story, build relationships with the media who tell it for you.

KRAIG'S LIST

3 THINGS: Why Media Relations Matter

A,B,C'S OF SUCCESS: Good media coverage starts and ends with the word "relations."

COVERAGE IS CURRENCY: If you invest in them, they'll invest in you.

ALLIES ARE HUGE: Media coverage in tough times is more important than in good times.

KANN LEADERSHIP

CHAPTER TWELVE
Media Relationships To Win

Value to Them Means Value for YOU

Never undervalue the power of the pen or the magnitude of the voice. Media shapes the perception of people, organizations and events. They always get the final word and it's your job to value their presence.

To date, I have had the great fortune to spend more than thirty years interviewing athletes and coaches in various sports at the collegiate and professional level. Dealing with big name athletes at events like the Super Bowl and the NBA All-Star game, Major League Baseball and the NHL playoffs gave me chills when I was doing local sports. With longtime ties to golf, I've covered or talked about just about every tour professional you could name. And a lot more you couldn't!

On the college athletics front, it was a thrill to chase the news and deliver stories on teams and schools during my various stops in local market news.

I was up close and personal with teams at Missouri, Auburn, Georgia, Miami, Florida, Florida State, Michigan, Michigan State, Notre Dame and Western Michigan.

I also spent time featuring student-athletes at high schools and even more on smaller college campuses like Hope College, Grand Valley State and Kalamazoo College – all in Michigan.

From my earliest days, I always made it a point to see how I was looked upon and treated as a member of the media by the organizations I covered and the athletes or executives I was reporting on. I felt it was important to build a solid reputation and be looked upon favorably.

My goal was always to make a positive connection – which I talked about in the last chapter.

If you're on the other side looking for good press and some attention – in this case the company, organization, team or even small business entrepreneur – you need to value the media in advance of any expectation you might have.

If you subscribe to the theory that in everything there is something to be gained, then you might want to look more closely at the media and what it might bring to your table in a positive way.

Today's media is far bigger than your father's, or grandfather's. Sure, newspapers are shrinking and other outlets are closing up shop. But the scope of attention has ramped up as today's media is filled with far more than just newspaper journalists, columnists, magazine writers and television and radio reporters and analysts.

Back in the 80's there wasn't a mad dash each day to surf the internet, let alone read someone's blog. And back in the 90's you'd have far better access to a smoking lounge before you'd ever stumble upon a chat room or social media café.

Indeed, today's world is moving faster than anyone could have imagined. It's a challenge to stay away from news or media forms available on our phone. Everyone has a phone and all it takes is a picture or a video posted to a social media site and it instantly becomes shareable content.

A Nielsen based report in 2019 showed that the number of adults in the United States who now watch television with a "smart phone" in hand or within arm's length is pushing almost 75%. Media content is everywhere and people are consuming it in alarming numbers.

And that's why this all matters.

Don't be so quick to dismiss the importance of the next interview or the next creative way to writing your company's press release.

Here are five things that media exposure (large or small doses) provides for you or your company.

- **A chance to be deemed interesting** – In today's world, being "un-interesting" means you haven't done much. No company wants that title and no person wants to be stuck among the ordinary. The stakes are simply too high.
- **A chance to become newsworthy** – In today's world, there's the link to good news and the attachment to some really bad news. I'd assume we're all working toward being known for something positive. Positive news results in positive gains for the brand and many would pay handsomely for a few minutes under a favorable media spotlight.
- **A chance to spread your story or your message** – In today's world of "likes," "re-tweets" and videos gone "viral," people want to see their content spread far and wide. A good interview, a creative press conference or being involved in a lively debate or televised forum is a great chance to spread the news about your group's efforts or your personal successes.
- **A chance to create and grow a following** – In today's world where Twitter has become as mainstream as McDonald's, every person has become (or has the chance to become) an individual brand providing value or valued content. Those who succeed are those who refuse to sit silent. Again, ask yourself a question those who dislike gossip would hate; "What are people saying about me?" Let the media or your next media opportunity become a way to create positive chatter.

- **A chance to do good, become a role model** — In today's world, it seems people are quick to anoint someone as a "role model." We're also just as quick to criticize those we've put on a pedestal. I'm not saying to put yourself out there as a role model. That's for others to decide. Instead, I'm suggesting that those doing good work or achieving great success are able to find their way into the media more easily and media opportunities provide avenues for valued recognition.

All five things mentioned above are nicely packaged under the biggest thing the media does, which is: *provide relevance.*

Each day people and corporations sit around trying to figure out their next move, or their next venture to new heights. Can media a part of that growth plan? I'd suggest they're certainly thinking about that.

Do you like the coverage you're getting? Make sure they know it. If you don't like the coverage you're getting, maybe you need to work harder at what you're putting in front of them.

So, how does all this apply to media relationships?

If media can provide all those things, then isn't time to consider the gain from building relationships with outlets and their reporters and making their efforts to cover you a bit easier?

The media world today is a mad scramble. Reporters are being asked to do a lot more. It's not just about the article that will be written. It's about a video clip they can also produce and perhaps two or three other assignments they are dealing with on a given day. Media want to go where they are valued. Many times, there is a choice to be made about what to cover and how much space they'll give it. Often times, it comes down to the ease of covering *you.*

With that, when it comes to taking your brand to another level or finding a way to get your story out to the masses, its officially time to consider putting the media on your branding checklist and find a few ways to make some friends with those carrying the microphone or the pad and pen.

If you want to win with your story, remember, its relationships that help shape the message and stories that are ultimately told.

KRAIG'S LIST

3 THINGS: Keys To Earned Media

RELATIONSHIPS: Build them and they will come. Show them you really care.

INVOLVEMENT: Include 'em in your biggest news days or promotional events.

MERCHANDISE: Promote the best stories tied to your organization and its news or people.

KANN LEADERSHIP

MY STORY

THE GOLF CHANNEL

Teeing Up My Greatest Opportunity

In the fall of 1994, I was sitting in the sports office at WWMT-TV in Kalamazoo, getting ready for the night's sportscast when the phone rang. It was a call from my television agent. His name was David Crane and he and his wife ran their own boutique agency.

It's pretty common for those in local television to find someone who's primary business is to peddle tapes to news directors around the country and help news, sports and weather anchors and reporters find their way up the ladder. Nobody graduates from school and suddenly has an agent eager to help them. At least nobody I knew!

It takes a few years, at least one job, and a few cracks at making a decent "me reel" to get the attention of an agent who sees a future for you and a reason to take a chance on you.

Agents take your best work, compile it into a resume tape - now an emailable and downloadable link - and send it along to news directors or television executives in hopes of landing you the interview for the next job along your career path. Typically, they'll take a commission on the contract you receive from the station of between six and ten percent of your salary each year. Early on, when you're making peanuts in the business, you're hesitant to part with your hard-earned wage. But you'll quickly find out that if you want to get somewhere special, you'll need a skilled and connected promoter - if you can get one. The money spent becomes a sound investment.

This wasn't the first call I'd received. I had some interest from top twenty-five media markets for various roles that included a mix of anchoring and reporting. Among the intriguing opportunities and landing spots was a station in Jacksonville but research in the form of a few phone calls around the business told me that I might not enjoy the head of the sports department who I'd be working alongside and that was a red flag. At least a strong yellow.

This particular call was different.

The call was to gauge my interest in a start-up network devoted to golf.

As the call went, this cable network was going to be called The Golf Channel.

A Prized Golf Channel Keepsake

It was linked to Arnold Palmer and a man named Joe Gibbs. Whenever I tell people that Joe Gibbs was involved, the immediate responses is something like, "Joe Gibbs? The football coach?" The answer is "no."

Joe was an entrepreneur from Alabama and he had a vision to take the game where it had never been before. He was an impressive and very likeable businessman who wanted to present golf, in all of its forms, to the masses, twenty-four hours a day.

The network was set to launch in January of 1995 and they were in search of on-air talent along with producers, directors, editors, videographers, studio engineers and every form of office management from human resources to sales executives. It was all going to happen fast!

As my agent David Crane put it, they had an interest in me as a field reporter and anchor for its flagship show which would be called *Golf Center*. Yes, *Golf Center*. (Later that was changed to *Golf Central* to stay away from a similarity to ESPN's *SportsCenter*. Crane was impressed by what he had heard and after sending my tape to Orlando, he was pretty excited that they were impressed with what they'd seen from my reel. So was I, to say the least!

Golf Channel Co-Founders Joe Gibbs and Arnold Palmer

With regard to whether I was going to go on the interview, it didn't take me long to say "yes." And before you knew it, I was on my way (very quietly) from Kalamazoo to Orlando to meet with a man named Mike Whelan. The truth of the story is that they flew me down in a first-class seat and back in coach. People always laugh at that, but it's true.

Whelan was a shortish man with a big personality and certainly confident. As he sat back in his chair peppering me with questions about my background in television and my interest and vision of covering golf as a full-time career, Whelan quickly impressed me. He had an element of "cool," a touch of ego and a no-nonsense way about him that was magnetic. He had come from HBO, had a cutting-edge style in how he wanted things done and would be the man in charge, running production for the network from the studio to the live remote team that would televise golf tournaments from coast to coast.

He sold me. He did it because he made it clear he had confidence in me. He told me I was someone who could help do the hard work necessary to launch the network and keep it on track with passionate reporting, delivering the news with credibility. He said I had something in me that he was ready to bet on. I was honored and internally pinching myself that this was really happening.

He offered me the job on the spot. The Golf Channel was one of the very first subscription networks with a sole focus on one sport and Whelan and his team were ready to hire its opening band of reporters and hosts. I was blown away at the thought.

Guess how long I had to make a decision?

I stood at a payphone on International Drive in Orlando at a *Chili's*. I remember it well. I told my wife that I'd just been offered the job and she said, "Great, come on home and let's talk about it all." My answer was pretty funny. "Sounds great," I said. "Except there's a catch. They've only given me 24-48 hours to make up my mind."

Original 1995 Golf Central Team with VP of Production Michael Whelan

We had some quick thinking to do, but I think we both knew what was going to happen.

How could you pass on the chance to be a part of something with Arnold Palmer's name attached to it? I'd been covering golf since the first job I took out of college and had grown to love it. I knew the sport, played the sport and was fascinated by the opportunity of being an "original cast member" at a new network.

The obvious potential downfall was that the network wouldn't make it. Even so, I figured that if The Golf Channel failed, my resume and resume tape would look far better than what I'd had going into the job.

A two-year contract landed in my lap with an opportunity to be part of something that had never been done and just like that, the first house that we'd bought just a couple months earlier had a for sale sign in front of it.

I remember walking into WWMT-TV news director Mike Rindo's office to break the news about me leaving for the Sunshine State and The Golf Channel. He said, "The GULF Channel?" I guess he thought I might be heading out to cover politics and war given current developments in our country, but I assured him it was GOLF not GULF and filled him in on the rest.

Rindo was a really good man, a great boss and gave me the chance to do far more than I was originally hired to do. I had gone from weekend sports anchor to basically splitting the weekday sports anchor role with John Koch and together we built a nice following and established ourselves as a strength within the station's news department.

Leaving Channel 3 in Kalamazoo was actually more difficult than you would think. I liked the neighborhoods and I felt it would be a perfect community to raise a family. I also liked that it was only a two-hour drive to Chicago, which was home for me. And, I liked the people in West Michigan – a lot.

Orlando was different. I remember thinking how big the city was during my time at *WINK* in Ft. Myers driving up to cover the expansion Orlando Magic back in the early 1990's. Now, I was living there full time and I was right in Arnold Palmer's back yard working in a network studio with people from varying backgrounds and established networks. Multiple people had left ESPN to join the Golf Channel venture. We had others from FOX and HBO and some had come from big city markets and others from regional networks.

The original studio on-air team became as close as any group I'd worked with. Can you name them?

Here is the roster – each played a key role in building the original Golf Channel brand.

- *Brian Hammons* – an Indianapolis guy who was and is as smooth as anyone I'd worked with. Our families spent time together and he and I co-hosted some of the earliest on-site coverage at majors.
- *Lynda Cardwell* – she was Brian's co-host on *Golf Central.* A southern lady with a great smile, Lynda was a friend to everyone, launched the first ever show with Brian and had a strong passion for her opportunity.
- *Jennifer Mills* – like me, she was one of the original PGA TOUR beat reporters and co-hosted with Hammons for a long time. Jennifer paid great attention to detail, was super competitive and a hard worker beyond what I saw from almost any woman I'd worked with in the business.
- *Mike Ritz* – the first on-air talent in the building. A loveable guy with a fantastic voice who was a really good golfer. I think we all learned a few things from him about the game and he had a confidence about him and the way he knew the game that carried him.
- *Tom Nettles* – a college football player in San Diego with a golf background just as strong. Tom was an athlete and former sportscaster in the Bay Area. Best sun tan in the business and a great laugh to go along with a funny temper. Everyone loved Nettles – at least I think they did.
- *Dwayne Ballen* – a South Carolina guy who previously worked local television in Raleigh and didn't stay In Orlando long. He was a polished pro who carried himself like a network newsman. Sharp dresser and

well versed, he was the original host of *Golf Today* – the pre-game show that aired each day before coverage came on the air.

- *Peter Kessler* – easily the most recognizable figure as he hosted the popular *Golf Talk Live* series from the moment the network launched. Kessler had the booming voice and a confidence I'd never seen. That rubbed many the wrong way. Kessler had all the guests and all the knowledge of the game. And he'd tell you so. That said, he made a very big impact and drew a following that the channel needed.

There were others who stood out as our analysts. Longtime PGA TOUR veteran Mark Lye on the men's side and a former player named Deborah Vidal on the women's side provided their insights. Lye was a long-timer and Vidal was a short-timer. Gary Smith and veteran writer George White added their color to the team.

Most impressive to me was the leadership.

At the start, it was a small company that felt like a big family. Whelan had a sidekick in Paul Fansworth and both spent a lot of time talking things over in the office of Bob Greenway. Farnsworth was fun-loving, Greenway was almost like the father-figure of the production team. He had respect of many and certainly me.

Producer Jeff Hymes came from the NBC family to lead *Golf Today* – we called it "Golf Today, Gone Tomorrow" – because ratings weren't the best in the early days and the show was ultimately put on the shelf. The show itself was terrific and it would come back years later as *Golf Central Pre-Game.* Mark Friedman was our other lead studio producer and manned the ship on *Golf Central* in the early days, taken over later by Hymes. Each was a good newsman and knowledgeable about the game and doing shows the right way.

The man who made the schedules go for all of us was a fun-loving, easy going guy from ESPN named Mike Stinton. He had to deal with all the satellite issues as we sent back our features from various tournaments and he had the job of coordinating which of us was heading out to which event.

The Hymes-Stinton office was the epicenter of both important and useless chat. It was always a good spot to go when you needed a break from writing scripts about the day's play at the John Deere Classic. More importantly, it was the hub of schedule politics because everyone was jockeying to get Stinton's ear about being the chosen reporter at a great spot like Hilton Head Island or whatever event was in your home town. And nothing was more important than waiting to see who was selected to cover each major championship.

Keith Hirshland was brought in by Whelan to oversee Live Tournament golf and he put together a terrific team. To me, what really stood out was the team Hirshland helped put together *behind* the camera. Folks like Pete Esposito, Jeff Gershengorn, Daisy Phipps and Jonathan Schwartz were as vital to the success of the events as on-air personalities like Donna Caponi and Jim Nelford who teamed with Denny Schreiner on various LPGA and PGA TOUR events.

I could write an entire book about Golf Channel. Hirshland has.

Here's a fact about the brand itself. In 1995, it was launched as The Golf Channel. Less than ten years later, it was rebranded as simply Golf Channel. For the sake of consistency, the rest of the way, I will probably just refer to it as Golf Channel or the Golf Channel, so don't be confused.

No matter what it was called and what the logo looked like, the stories we could all tell would be enough for a ten-book series. Instead, I'll share my highlights and my thoughts on some topics and some of the people you may know attached to my time at "Golf's Channel."

Majors

- My first great opportunity came in 1995. Soon after Arnold Palmer and Joe Gibbs flipped the switch on January 17th, we were already focused on the channel's first big major. Mike Ritz and I drew the assignment as reporters for the Masters that year – ultimately won by Ben Crenshaw. How lucky was I? I'll never forget my first drive down famed Magnolia Lane and watching the people scamper to put down their chairs around the eighteenth hole. Everything was green and everything was perfect. In fact, that was the first story I did that week. "Everything is green." We covered that tournament like a glove. On Sunday morning, I drew the lucky straw that I'd won a lottery spot among media people chosen to play the course on Monday morning after the tournament. We weren't allowed any warm up balls on the range and I had to start my round on the 10th hole. I was in heaven for five hours. I had a caddie and a yardage book that let me plot my way around the course, marking an "x" by every spot. For the record, Amen Corner comes up really quick when you start on number 10! I shot 88 that day with a lone birdie and more than a few 3-putts on greens faster than I'd ever played.
- I was at Shinnecock Hills a few months later when Corey Pavin launched his miraculous fairway wood into the 18th hole to win the U.S. Open. That same year, I was also lucky enough to get a trip to Hawaii for the *Grand Slam of Golf* to see Crenshaw, Pavin, John Daly and Steve Elkington tee it up as the major winners that year. My first ever trip to Hawaii.
- Among the other major champions I witnessed up close; Jose Maria Olathabal, Mark O'Meara, Mike Weir and Angel Cabrera at Augusta, Shaun Micheel at Oak Hill, Vijay Singh's PGA Championship wins at Sahalee and Whistling Straights, David Toms and Keegan Bradley's

PGA's Atlanta Athletic Club, the win by Mark Brooks in 1996 at Valhalla, Tom Lehman at the 1996 Open Championship, Jim Furyk at Olympia Fields and Cabrera's triumph at Oakmont. Maybe most impressive was the landslide win by Rory McIlroy at the U.S. Open held at Congressional Country Club. There were others, but those stand out. I'll get to the one that trumps them all in a bit.

Ryder Cups

- If you haven't been, you need to go. It's worth every dollar. I was fortunate beyond words to have covered the first overseas Ryder Cup for Golf Channel. Brian Hammons and I made the trip to Valderrama, Spain with a terrific producer named Eric Saperstein and our top-notch video crew, Al Pollock and Paul Schlegel - which we'll remember as the week that Seve Ballesteros made history on home soil and also as the major that included drives to and from the hotel of more than two hours each way and stops for food at gas stations. At the time, Golf Channel didn't have a lot of pull when it came to top notch nearby hotels.
- I don't know if there was ever an atmosphere as electric as what we saw in Louisville when Captain Paul Azinger used Valhalla as his personal playground for a new "pod system" - breaking his team into practice and playing partnerships - he employed to win the Cup for the United States. I was there hosting *Live From.* One word – amazing.

Arnold Palmer

- The King was as good as advertised. To be a part of his network was a dream and also an honor I took very seriously. He had his own parking space at the studio which was a cool sight to see every day. When he made trips into the studio to check on his investment, everyone seemingly stopped. He always made us feel special. He made it a point to call people by name and he remembered many of us. But nothing was more special for me than a trip with Arnie to Conyers, Georgia soon after the Olympics were staged in Atlanta in 1996. Arnold was opening a new golf course and I was dispatched with cameraman Al Pollock to document the day. When I was told we'd fly with Mr. Palmer on his plane up and back, I about thought I'd done it all. He piloted the plane while Al and I sat comfortably a few rows back with

Flying with The King

his late wife Winnie. She was going to take the plane to the Carolinas after we were dropped in Georgia to see after their furniture business. What I remember most, was scurrying back to the plane after Mr. Palmer finished his round, only to see him standing atop the jet stairs and telling us to hurry up! When The King was ready, he was ready. Once we landed back in Orlando and pulled into his private hangar, I remember telling him thank you for a wonderful day and then starting to make my way down the steps and out to my car. What happened next is one of my greatest professional memories.

"Hey boys," he said almost puzzled that we were leaving. "Where are you headed?!" "Home, Mr. Palmer," was my respectful reply.

He would have nothing of it.

"The hell you are! Let's have a beer," was his follow up and with that I made a call home to notify my wife that when The King says we're having a beer, you simply just have a beer. It was a thrill.

Presidents

- One of the great things about being at *Golf Channel* in the earliest days was simply being a part of the novelty. It was something special for everyone - including our country's leaders. Along the way, I had the chance to interview the likes of Presidents Gerald Ford, George W. Bush, his father George H.W, Bush (who actually helped usher Golf Channel onto the air with a good luck salute from the Oval Office in 1995) and Bill Clinton. What stands out is my first trip to the White House – representing the Golf Channel as a guest of President George W. Bush and First Lady Laura Bush. Soon after the tragic events of Hurricane Katrina, I was selected to interview Mrs. Bush in New Orleans during the week of the city's PGA TOUR event. The First Lady had played a prominent role in assisting relief efforts for area schools and libraries and the Golf Channel and CBS were given sit-down opportunities to discuss her passion for the project. The extensive background checks the White House did on me before that interview were nothing short of amazing. Long phone calls and lots of questions! As I tell people, when we sat down together for the interview, I felt like she knew as much about me as I knew about me!

  A few months later, an invitation arrived to my mailbox at Golf Channel, giving me the opportunity to bring my wife to the White House holiday reception for the media as guests of President Bush and the First Lady. Wow! As I found out later, a perk of doing an exclusive sit down with the President or First Lady in a calendar year resulted in an invitation to spend an evening in December at the White House. Lucky me and we had a blast. Rubbing shoulders with the likes of Bob

Schieffer, Wolf Blitzer, Chris Wallace and others was a thrill ride that tops any amusement park. And the great thing about the night was that those men wanted to talk about golf with me! Amazing how big the sport can be sometimes and how being a part of Golf Channel gave me a link to so many celebrities.

Tiger Woods

When Tiger leapt to the professional circuit after his run of U.S. Amateur titles, the Golf Channel took a big leap too. My opportunities to cover arguably the greatest player ever to play the game were long and eventful.

Tracking Tiger Woods – Hoylake, England

- His "Hello World" press conference took place in Milwaukee at the Greater Milwaukee Open and I was the Golf Channel's reporter on site that week. To this day, I stump people with the trivia question about the other two players he was grouped with for his first two rounds. The answer, by the way, is Jeff Hart and John "Jumbo" Elliott. Tiger didn't win but he did make deafening noise with a hole-in-one that week and we were off to the races.
- In '97, I was on-site for the Masters when Woods broke through for his first green jacket. I was given the assignment of interviewing Woods one-on-one in a locker room sit-down reserved for ESPN, Golf Channel and CNN. I'll never forget it.
- I was there for a few of his other Augusta wins as well, and was the host of *Live From* at Southern Hills in Tulsa, Oklahoma on what was the hottest major championship in my memory. As my good friend and PGA TOUR winner Steve Flesch would say, it was like playing golf on the face of the sun. Obviously, I didn't compete, but wearing a suit and make-up under television lights was hardly comfortable to begin with, let alone factoring in temperatures that soared above 100 degrees.
- I was there at Hoylake when Woods won the Open Championship shortly after the passing of his father, Earl. I covered that emotional victory with Rich Lerner – one of the best I've ever worked with at capturing the essence of a win and painting the clear story of how a major championship really felt.

- In 2008, I was the host of *Live From* at Torrey Pines when Woods pulled off the unthinkable – winning the U.S Open in a Monday playoff on a broken leg.
- I was there soon after for Tiger's epic collapse. Not on the golf course, but off. I just happened to be the lone anchor in the studio the day after Thanksgiving when Tiger had a run-in with a fire hydrant that changed his own course. As I like to say, it was mayhem, madness and yet, a mission that every anchor or news reporter wants to be a part of at some time. What started as a report with few details, turned into the story of the year in sports and beyond.
- I was in the studio when he held his big nationally televised mea culpa press conference in February of 2010.

Along the way, I realized that whether it was up close from the fairway, up above from the set of *Live From* shows, or in studio show meetings with Brandel Chamblee, Frank Nobilo, writer Brian Hewitt, Peter Oosterhuis and others, Tiger Woods really was golf during that time. Unless you really truly lived it, you just don't know how big a figure Tiger was and how golf changed by the week and the year because of him. We all learned in real time just how the Golf Channel had escalated because of him. Many people have criticized Woods, but few have lived the world of covering him day after day. For those who didn't and never will, I will tell you that as much as many have questioned the massive doses of coverage directed his way, the interest in everything he did and how he did it dictated the direction of show content. It still does and as long as he is still playing, it always will.

Golf Channel & Golf Personalities

I've been asked so many times about so many people I have worked with.

People want to know this and that about everyone and what they are like, who's nice, who's not etc. I will say right up front that I don't get into that game and never have.

Television is a very tough – yet interesting – business and to arrive at any level of notoriety is a real challenge. Staying there is more difficult. I'd like to believe that everyone below is a friend and a respected colleague.

So, for you true golf fans reading this book, here are a few more quick thoughts on some folks I've mentioned already. And some thoughts as well on other talents I haven't mentioned yet and have truly been blessed to work with. Each has their own "brand" for sure and here's how I spin it on each of them.

- *Frank Nobilo* – After a long Golf Channel run, Frank is now at CBS Sports on their golf team. I covered Frank when he was a world class player. I interviewed him in back-to-back years when he won the *Sarazen World Open* outside Atlanta. Then I got to work with him. You will not find a classier man in the television industry. His commentary comes not just from his head, but his heart. It's gold. I consider him the best golf television man I've ever worked with.

Original LIVE FROM on Site with Brandel Chamblee & Frank Nobilo

- *Brandel Chamblee* – Nobilo, Chamblee and I traveled the post-game show and then the *Live From* show from its very first days. Nobody puts in more effort than Brandel. People think he's a lightning rod and I always laugh when people criticize him. Not one thing comes from his mouth that he hasn't put the time in to think about. What makes him great is that he doesn't have six majors on his resume. He knows golf is hard, he has massive respect for the game and he gives you the proper perspective that it isn't easy to succeed. He holds the biggest names to the highest standard of excellence which is bold. Major respect from me. He also likes chips, salsa and guacamole at least as much as I do.
- *Peter Oosterhuis* – You want a kind soul who was great at the game and had an endearing way about him on and off camera? Peter treated everyone like a friend. He made CBS telecasts unique with his voice and he elevated the Golf Channel shows by simply being "Oosty." I was offered the opportunity to co-emcee his charity event a few years back with the great Jim Nantz. Talk about an honor. Two of golf's nicest men. I put it on my highlight list.
- *Mark Rolfing* – "Mr. Hawaii" is another of the men that joined the team when NBC and Golf Channel locked business arms and he, too, instantly made us better. Rolf (as everyone calls him) doesn't have a bucket-load of PGA TOUR wins but for my liking, he calls golf like he has two buckets. I've never seen or heard Mark say a bad thing about anyone. That's worth a lot.
- *Jerry Foltz* – Jerry likes to give me credit for helping him rise rise through the ranks at Golf Channel. Maybe a few need a bump, but most people make their own breaks. That's what Jerry did. Ask former live golf producer Keith Hirhsland – a star talent himself – who gave Jerry the rope to find

his way. "Foltzy" is the greatest example of a guy who wasn't a world-beater with clubs in hand, but found his niche with a microphone in it and is perhaps the most relatable golf commentator you will find. He's a star, he just doesn't know it.

- *David Feherty* – As smart as he is funny. As kind as he is quirky. His career has skyrocketed and when he first came on board to make some appearances, it would have been easy for the (then CBS) commentator to "big time" everyone. Exactly the opposite. I remember a morning at the U.S. Open at Congressional won by Rory McIlroy. I came into the television compound only to find Feherty crashed out on the couch, lying flat and sound asleep. When he woke up, he let us all know that he'd gotten a bit lost on his way home to the hotel the night before. Feherty had ridden his bike, lost his way and turned what was about seven miles into about forty-seven! He said he'd gotten back to the hotel after 3am. Only Feherty could do it and only he could tell it the way he did.
- *Mark Lye, Curt Byrum and Donna Caponi* – I've grouped them together because as a collective group they helped me find my way doing play-by-play for three years. Lye always asked me "what are we coming out of the box with?" Byrum had all of his ties pre-tied and made me laugh more than anyone I worked with on the live golf team. To me, he's easily the most underrated golf commentator there is. Donna was a star LPGA player and as comfortable to work with as anyone you could have found. She was really the Golf Channel's "first lady" and they couldn't have found a better one.
- *Steve Sands* – Steve was a local sportscaster like me who had found his way from local sports in Orlando to Golf Channel as a reporter and anchor. He found his way pretty quickly and has now become a staple of the golf team at NBC *Sports* – basically graduating from Golf Channel. Sands is smooth and smart. He found his niche as an interviewer and I honestly don't know if there is a better one in golf, maybe sports television across the board.
- *Todd Lewis* – Todd sat in front of me for a handful of years at Golf Channel. Like Sands, Lewis came from the Orlando market as a reporter and anchor. He and Steve basically followed the same path. Todd has my respect more for the person he is than all the talent he has. He always cares about doing the right thing and treating people the right way. If you get to meet him, do it. You'll be glad you did.
- *Scott Van Pelt* – Where do we begin? Easily the most famous "graduate" of The Golf Channel. He wasn't among the original on-air team at the network, but he was – and is – an original. He climbed the ranks from production assistant to reporter and anchor. Scott, Jennifer Mills and

I rotated as PGA TOUR beat reporters for a few years and when we weren't on the road at a tournament, we sat next to mainstay Brian Hammons on the *Golf Central* set. I anchored a lot of shows with Scott. We hosted a few majors together as well including Vijay Singh's win at Sahallee outside Seattle in 1998. I'll speak in the present tense because it applies to the past. He is witty, funny, thoughtful and creative. To me, Scott's greatest strength is his willingness to go off-script, have fun and connect with an audience. I have huge respect for what he's accomplished because he didn't take the "local news path" like many of us did. He had people laughing in the studio when he was laughing himself and also when he was angry. Van Pelt is a gem and a darned good human being who always seemed to care about people and their families. I'm glad for his success.

- *Vince Cellini* – One of my best friends in the business and somebody I learned a lot from. To this day we laugh about the day he came to the Golf Channel. Vince was the first "big name" to join our team, having spent time as a mainstay on CNN as a host of *Sports Tonight*. I'll never forget a member of our Golf Channel on-air team being less than enthused about him joining the mix, fearing that it meant less opportunity for them and maybe turning the spotlight on a new person. I told them they were crazy. Cellini's addition gave us added credibility, made our line-up even stronger and sent a message to industry folks that the Golf Channel was a great place to be. We became fast friends. On his first day, I heard he was over at his new desk filling out papers and meeting people so I rolled in and in a loud voice yelled, "Hey, where the &? %$ is Cellini?!" He laughed and I think it made him feel welcome. He is as smooth as they come, feisty for sure but always has the best product in mind and wants people to succeed. To me, he was the most important hire made during my time at Golf Channel.
- *Kelly Tilghman* – I co-anchored her first ever *Golf Central* show. She was nervous but yet had a confidence that was impressive. Kelly played collegiately at Duke, knew the game and found her way to Golf Channel as a production assistant in the video library. She didn't have the local news background like many but she had the drive to learn television, the work ethic to see her way past mistakes we all made in local markets, and the look that made viewers give her a shot. She got her start as an on-course reporter during live tournaments thanks to our lead production executive at the time, Don McGuire – a well-respected former Turner executive who came to Golf Channel with ideas and experience. He saw something in her and she made the most of it. Kelly became a *Golf Channel* favorite in a very short time

and later became the surprise choice to lead the channel into the new television contract with the PGA TOUR as its primary voice next to Nick Faldo. Many were shocked. Kelly worked her tail off to prove them wrong. That's the biggest thing I can say about someone who I sat next to and watched succeed; she never took things for granted and worked to make a name for herself. That she did.

I could talk about so many more because people came and went. Our cast included really fun guys like former ESPN anchor Iain Page who could break into a great Hubie Brown impersonation at a moment's notice, serious journalists like Adam Barr, and others who came with nice resumes like Inga Hammond. I also spent a few really good years on the Golf Central desk partnering with Megan West, now officially Megan Mullen. The wife of successful college football coach Dan Mullen, she joined our team in 2005 and brought a fun energy to our show along with being one of the most positive, selfless people I'd ever come across in the business. Dan's coaching rise and a young family altered her career path, but we've remained great friends beyond the television studio. I also worked alongside Gary Williams and Erik Kuselias who launched *Morning Drive* . I was their fill-in when one of them took time off.

In my time at Golf Channel, I hosted almost everything. While *Golf Central* was my original role, I also put on an apron and hosted an equipment show called *Golf Channel Workshop* with a man named Bob Dodds. It was actually pretty fun, and yet I still don't know how to re-grip my own clubs. I hosted a show named *Viewer's Forum* which was a Sunday night phone in show after the tournament play was over. We took calls and batted around topics on a panel with established golf writers as the primary analyst. I hosted *Leaderboard Report* – a weekly wrap-up show specifically designed to roll full leaderboards and pour through interesting tournament tid-bits. I filled in on *Golf Talk Live*, found myself in the rotation on *College Central,* and spent a lot of time hosting *Academy Live* and *School of Golf.*

Original Golf Channel Post Game with Brian Hewitt & Mark Lye

Instructional shows were fun. But let me tell you, it can turn your handicap upside down in a hurry! I went from a 4.5 index to about a 9 in a matter of a few shorts years thanks to listening to new tips each week. Gullible? Guilty as charged.

People expected you to be a really good player if you worked at Golf Channel. I'm not. I've shot 73 on multiple occasions but could just as easily shoot 84. My best round is the 74 I posted at Whistling Straights in Kohler,

Wisconsin with three Golf Channel witnesses. Thankfully, I had David Kamens and my boss, Tony Tortorici along that day or nobody would believe that I made everything that day, and played the wind like I knew what I was doing.

I have so many memories.

A few shows stood out among my favorites.

I hope the true golf fan remembers a show modeled after ESPN's *"Around the Horn"* called *The Approach with Callaway Golf.* Former PGA TOUR winner Andrew Magee let it fly from a golfer's perspective and Alex Miceli, a longtime golf writer who was known to have opinions and also get under people's skin, took aim from the media side while I judged their answers. That show was a hoot.

For me, *The Grey Goose 19th Hole* was even better. I sat in the middle of a panel-filled couch of between three and five and moderated a fast-paced opinion-based show that was half drama and probably half comedy to tee up the golf each week. The regular cast included golf scribes Jeff Rude and John Hawkins who played their roles marvelously, tossing jabs at one another while also strategically and picking sides on controversial topics.

Those were the shows I enjoyed most, along with covering majors from *the Live From* set.

In my time at Golf Channel, I had the pleasure of covering a lot of big-time events. Frankly, I lost count and probably couldn't tally the number. As great as it was to be on site at the biggest events in the sport, my memories are the people and the connections I made through the game.

It was like a traveling circus for non-Tour guys like me, Brian Hammons, Jennifer Mills, Rich Lerner, Steve Sands, Tim Rosaforte, Kelly Tilghman and others. We were treated like rock-stars by tournaments and fans. Players would actually laugh and give us grief when we would walk through the lines of people, stop, and actually sign autographs just like they did. It was an amazing feeling and a special thing to be a part of the game at the highest level. On the side, we played some of the great golf courses around the country thanks to clubs, courses and their staff of professionals who welcomed us with open arms. It was a pretty good life I'd say.

Do I have any regrets? Sure.

My greatest is that I didn't give play-by-play a longer run. A few years before I settled into a main studio role, I was fortunate to have Don Maguire believe in me enough to put me on the live tournament team as an on-course commentator. I wasn't a former pro like many who had that role, but he saw something and gave me the chance to be a part of lead producer Keith Hirshland's team.

I called golf shots and conducted interviews for a year before landing in the host seat on what was then the Buy.com Tour, later the Web.com Tour, and now the Korn Ferry Tour. I replaced television veteran Denny Schreiner who was the network's first play-by-play voice. At that time, Golf Channel didn't own the rights to the PGA TOUR's early round coverage and we only had about thirty events total spread among the various tours including the LPGA and even the Canadian Tour.

It was a thrill. I was honored.

But it was a lot of travel. Of the events we had, I did little more than half and shared time with Grant Boone, a good friend blessed with one of the best broadcast voices I'd heard. It was around 2003 when Hirshland and production head Tony Tortorici asked me into an office and said they wanted to have "one voice" and talked to me about potentially doing all thirty or so of the live tournaments.

Flattered would be an understatement. I respected Hirshland a lot. I worked with a few live tournament producers at the major networks and Keith was easily on par and in some cases beyond.

The job would have been amazing but there was a drawback.

I asked what I'd be doing the other twenty-two weeks out of the year and the answer gave me pause. It was what led me to my decision.

On non-tournament road weeks, Tortorici said I'd be in the studio anchoring *Golf Central* from Wednesday to Sunday. That meant basically zero weekends with family. My twin boy Trent and girl Hailey were under the age of seven at the time and my youngest daughter Kendall was not quite three. I was torn. I wrestled with it for a few days and just couldn't do it.

Ultimately, I settled in the studio hosting Pre and Post Game coverage, *Golf Central* and other shows. And there wasn't a day that went by that I wasn't blessed and feeling fortunate for the opportunity to have such a prominent role alongside so many talented people. I realized the gift of being well-rounded which gave me the opportunity to have a choice. Many never get that. Some never get the chance to be a Little League baseball or softball coach either. Life is about choices.

With me in the studio, talented men like Boone and then Brian Anderson took over the play-by-play duties.

Anderson proved to be one of the best hires Golf Channel ever made. As good as he was, he didn't last long when Kelly Tilghman was anointed as the lead voice once the PGA TOUR's big contract came to the network.

Anderson, who had really made a mark with everyone on the staff, left for the lead television job with the Milwaukee Brewers which has led him to the Turner family of networks. He has become a rising star in baseball and basketball. He can do it all and he's as nice a man as they come in the industry.

People come and people go. That's the nature of the business. Very few have the staying power and very few get the choice to stay or go completely on their own terms.

So why did I ultimately leave Golf Channel in 2011?

It's complicated, yet fairly simple, I felt like life has a plan for you and sometimes your hand also gets forced a bit.

Television is a moving target. The "family atmosphere" of the little old network known as The Golf Channel from the start in 1995, had gone into the hands of cable television company Comcast in 2000. Things became more corporate and we could see it and feel it. It wasn't bad. It was just different.

In 2009, amidst another sea of change that had Comcast's Golf Channel heading toward the NBC Universal family, many folks were at risk. Contracts were up for a number of us and some made more money than others. I was one of those fortunate to be well compensated. Yet, the new management team had decisions to make.

Two years earlier, in 2007, I had an opportunity to sign a two-year contract or a four-year contract and I chose two. Not because I didn't see myself staying, but because I have always been the type that wants to know my role. Unfortunately, nobody could guarantee what I'd be doing three years or four years down the road.

Many people were let go in that crazy year that was 2009. Many of my personal on-air friends saw their contracts not renewed.

It was jarring and eye-opening to watch the new management team led by a man named Tom Stathakes shake things up – in my opinion, not much for the better. I say that, not because he wasn't qualified to make his own decisions, but because of the way it was carried out. His background was impressive and he had confidence that we were going to move in a great direction. But his style was rough around the edges and it never really gave many of us a sense of confidence. For some, in front of and behind the camera, our years of effort to grow the channel felt wiped away. That's just the truth.

My Start as an Entrepreneur – HTK MEDIA

It was a new day. Something you learn in many corporate situations and suddenly the friendly confines of the original Golf Channel felt very corporate. I'd say it was a sign of growth more than anything.

In July 2009, during the week of the Open Championship at Troon, I received an unexpected call from my agent at CSE who told me that I was "free to look around" as my contract would be renewed at its current rate. I'll never forget it.

It was a Thursday and I was in studio that day hosting *LIVE FROM* with Kelly Tilghman and ironically had my financial advisor and great friend Kent

Skornia coming to town for our annual pow wow. My, how the conversations changed. Neither of us saw it coming.

Long story short, by the end of the year, Stathakes had changed his tune and Golf Channel offered me a one-year deal at a reduced rate – still with the role as lead studio host. From here, I would be paid by the day, work four days a week and no longer have a benefits package as a full-time employee. It was a lot to digest. While grateful to be retained, the money issue was jarring to a family of five and the lack of benefits made no sense to me given the role I was being allowed to maintain.

I loved my job and while there were interview opportunities that would take the family elsewhere, the thought of uprooting everyone was tough to rationalize. Not to mention, we had just moved into a new house.

We made the decision to stay the course, and I made two important, life changing commitments to myself.

The first was that I would give my all like never before and have the best year ever on air in 2010. Not for Stathakes or for Golf Channel, but for me and my family and my career. I would not let the turn of events curb my energy or shake my confidence.

Second, I would use the extra day during the week not working at the Golf Channel to do something different. And that I did.

I quickly formed a Limited Liability Company for myself, called *HTK Media*. I would do consulting with folks on media and communications, media coaching for athletes and executives and I would also jump on the speaking circuit to cash in on opportunities that I couldn't accept while Golf Channel basically owned my schedule as an employee.

HTK stood for "Have the Knowledge" and it was also the initials of my three children; Hailey, Trent and Kendall. As I figured, if it became what I wanted, years later I would want my kids to know that they were in my mind when I launched it.

I worked as hard at that as anything I had done. It was different and I was my own boss. I think I made fifty thousand dollars that first year. Nothing to get rich on, but I was proud.

Among other things, I landed an opportunity at the Southeastern Conference's Digital Network, run by XOS Digital in Orlando. I was a studio host there talking about college football, basketball and baseball.

To keep options open, my agent team at CSE kept me on the market. I interviewed with other networks with an eye on finding my value outside of the place I'd given my all to for the last fifteen or so years.

In June of 2011, after what I honestly believe were the two best years of my television career, something happened. It changed my focus, and it changed by career path. I was about to make the biggest pivot of my professional career.

Stay tuned.

CHAPTER THIRTEEN

Social Media Platforms To Win

Give Them Reason To Follow YOU

If you want people to follow you, then you'd better build platforms strong in value and give them something worth following.

Here's something for you.

According to a recent report by GlobalWebIndex, 98% of all people have at least one social network account. Maybe more interesting is the statistic that the average person has 7.6 active social media accounts.

As I write this book, data shows that more than 2.3 billion people worldwide are monthly participants on Facebook, almost 350 million have found their way to Twitter and a billion people are monthly active users on Instagram. The world's top business platform, LinkedIn, has now surpassed 650 million registered users.

Eye-popping? Get used to it. It's not slowing down. And that's me mentioning only a few of the platforms available.

From marketers to consumers and consumers to friends, social media is not a fraud. And it's far more than just a fad. It is now a big way of life.

Today, followers are like currency. People aren't satisfied by getting a few extra "likes," they now try to figure out how to get more. It's a game.

I look at social media like this; it's an opportunity to showcase who we are, what we're about and the value we are able to bring.

For me, until somebody decides it's a "pay per post" service or there's a cost to me for every view to my Twitter feed or my Instagram line-up, then I'm going to ride social media as fast and as far as I can.

My brand depends on it. So, too, does yours.

When I hear people say social media isn't for everyone, I smile. The statistics I've laid out show most everyone actually does find their way to some social media platform at some point or through someone they know. My current business is proof that it can help you share your story and also put more clients on your roster sheet and more revenue in your bank account.

I was at Golf Channel when Facebook launched on February 4, 2004 and when Twitter jumped in front of us in July of 2006. I remember scratching my head and wondering what life was coming to. Now, some tell me it's actually *become* my life!

They're joking. But, I'll admit that I spend quite a bit of time focusing on what I post, what I read, who I'm trying to reach and what my message is for the day or the week.

In my workshops, I begin by asking for a show of hands and asking the questions; "Who considers themselves a leader?" "Who wants to become a better leader?"

Everyone raises their hand.

Well, if life is truly about "leadership" then isn't a successful leadership template built around having a loyal following?

I believe it is. Getting those around you to follow your lead or support your efforts and offerings is as important as what you're working to accomplish.

In social media…building a "following" is everything. Today's marketing is completely different in all lines of work. Phone calls, billboards and marketing kits are ancient efforts as a solo strategy to create and maintain a dedicated client base. Everyone is seeking innovative ways to connect with people.

Today, if you don't have a worthy communication message, it's probably just somebody's spam. To gain traction, your worthy message must be communicated across new lines reaching new and different audiences.

I believe those who have something special to sell aren't always the most successful. It's those who actually sell themselves best that win. Social media is a great way to get the message out.

Author Jeffrey Gitomer - *"Social Boom"* - questions the importance of money earned as an important tie to being noticed or recognized. As he says, the new currency is quickly becoming "attention" – and that alone is what drives the majority of social media.

I get his message. Everyone wants attention for their successes and everyone who achieves success wants to build upon that and grow. To do that, you need people who follow your lead and those folks to spread the word about your success.

Social media should never be a hard push to sell. Turn people "on," not off, by delivering news, information or expertise that is always of value.

Here are 5 thoughts to keep in mind about social media if you want to grow your following:

- **At its core, social media means "being social"** — Don't just tell people what you're doing. Share the **experience** of what you're doing and show them what it feels like to take part in what you are doing. There's an emotional difference.

- **Have a "value message"** – If you don't provide things people care about or don't share enough details about you or your cause, you're probably nothing more than a quick delete or a spot in the junk file and you certainly won't grow a following. Value messages create interest and people will feel compelled to tell others.
- **Social media means sharing** – Sharing involves a strong level of trust and adds credibility to your brand if you're taking it seriously. Share what you feel good about, and what you'll feel confident about.
- **If you're working to create in individual brand, identify what you are all about** – Find out and identify what makes you unique among the many others "sharing" in social media. Then, build upon what makes you special.
- **Social media takes strategic work and a consistent presence** – The more you offer, the more impactful the message. The less you offer, the less likely anyone notices and the less chance anyone remembers it was you who offered it.

In short, I feel like those who reach success, create opportunities. Opportunities come from sharing what makes you special. Sharing something that creates an emotional connection leads to a bigger following. But as it grows, don't slow down. Stay consistent in putting yourself and your value out in the marketplace for consumption.

If you want to win with your story, focus on being better at what you do than others in your field and make sure your message is worth selling. The rest is all about the effort you put into your social media "brand" and the story people will see.

KRAIG'S LIST

3 THINGS: Basic Thoughts On Social Media

DON'T WAIT, JUMP IN: It's a free brand building opportunity. Yes, I said free.

STRATEGY WINS: Don't chase followers. Put out consistent value and they'll come.

WHO ARE YOU: Work to be known for something. You-nique content is valuable and shareable.

KANN
LEADERSHIP

CHAPTER FOURTEEN

Social Media Platforms To Win

It's Nobody's Business But YOURS

Should executives or corporate leaders be on social media sharing? Of course. Potential business partners live on social media, right? People want to see who's leading the brand.

Who's in? Who's not? Who's committed? Who has a plan? It's a big world out there with a whole lot of folks jockeying for position.

Personal brands and corporate brands. Athletes, executives, authors, reporters, speakers – ***everyone*** seemingly has something to say.

If your goal is to build your business, then dig in get to work on a social strategy designed to show people the value gained *because* of your business. In other words, don't just advertise you or the product itself. Work to give people valuable information and show people what associating with you - or your business - can add to their lives.

The best use of social media shouldn't be a hard push. Not for sales, not for personal or corporate financial gain, not for propaganda and certainly not for intentional and misguided self-promotion.

Any of the above has a decent chance at turning people off as they check your Facebook, Twitter, Instagram or any other social media space attached to you and your brand.

What is it that separates you from others in the same field? How is your business different than the competition? Answer those questions.

As it applies to me, there are many smart, uber experienced people who travel delivering "career development" seminars or workshops. My social media strategy isn't to tell people that's what I do as well. My goal is to showcase what it's like to be ***in*** my leadership workshop. I want people to have a window into the world of the *Kann Advisory Group* and its offerings which include the *Elevate Workshop.*

I focus on presenting the experience, and the emotion that goes with it, on my social media platforms. I don't just say "here's what I do." Pictures and videos that capture the feeling of being inside the experience are important to deliver on that.

Socially speaking, here's a few things to aim for in broadcasting your story. Remember, it's about the story of you and the story of your business. The hope, with each "tweet," post or blog, is to create or deliver one of the following:

- **A feeling of inclusion** – Everyone wants to feel "connected" these days. Social media, after all, means being *social.* So, try to make sure you work to include, connect and provide a real look at what you are all about.
- **Deliver relevant information** – Who isn't looking for help on something? Whether it's how to hook up your stereo system, the latest in fashion trends, or when might be a good time to tweet (try the noon hour), if you provide something people want, or something that's helpful, you've just made a valuable connection and earned the opportunity to gain their trust. Winning them over takes more time.
- **Provide a call to action** – People want inspiration beyond just entertainment. If they didn't, there wouldn't be a "speaker's bureau" as a hub for motivational speakers or a "job fair" that puts businesses out there to get people excited about their next career step. With your posts, think about what you want people to do after they see your social media message.

Is social media right for your business? Ask yourself if your business should be sharing what you do and who you are with the rest of the world. You'll find your answer.

Nobody scrolls down their Twitter feed without stopping on ***something.*** Very few zip through their news feed on Facebook without being held for at least a few seconds. The question becomes; what will you do to get people to stop on your post? And how will you then turn people onto your space?

It's like reading down the list of stocks in the paper. What stops you is what interests you. So, work within your social media platforms to make sure that when people see *you,* there's reason enough to stop and pay attention. Because if you turn them on to you, those folks may just turn others your way as well.

Here's an exercise; look at your last ten social media posts on any of your platforms. Analyze it and look closely.

What does it say about you? What does it suggest about your business or industry? Is there a trend? Does it suggest a consistent message or communicate exactly what you want people to know about you?

That string of posts is your brand. That is the story you are putting out for the world to see. That is what people will think of you and what also gives them the content that forms what they will share with others about you.

If you're comfortable with the posts, great. If it sends inconsistent messages, then it might be time to refocus your use of the platforms attached to your name.

I'm often asked by others who run a small business, or those in companies who've been clients about the impact social media has had on my own business.

There is no question that it's done great things for me. I've had leaders of organizations call me about my offerings after seeing a post. That leads to conversations about delivering something for their team and that turned into me hopping on a plane within a few weeks to present to their group. Perhaps most importantly, it's given my brand a spot in people's brains.

Being 'top of mind' for people who may someday want to engage is what I'm trying to create.

I want my story and the story of my business to come to mind for people when they are locked in conversations with others. I want them to consider me when looking to fill a speaking opportunity or a leadership workshop for their team. I want them to know that I'm in the space among leaders in a particular area.

Remember, if you don't put your brand out there, who knows that it even exists?

Here are three final things regarding social media as you look to find your own way in a space that can be a bit overwhelming.

- **The focus shouldn't be on talking about yourself**—It should be about connecting with others - through your experiences.
- **Don't use the social media platform to beg for a following**—The key is to how you use it to create a following based on your insights and shared ideas or opinions.
- **The bottom line is the build. Take the leap and take your time**—Do it one social media post at a time and create one theme tied to you and your brand that streams consistently above the others.

Wherever you choose put plant your flag, own your space. Then stay committed to delivering value to people on the receiving end.

There are a lot of people pushing out content. If you want to win with your story, make sure your messages aren't just content. Make sure they're something special and relevant. The followers will come.

KRAIG'S LIST

3 THINGS: Social Media As Your Advantage

HAVE A STORY: Who are you. What do you offer. Why do you do it.

SHARE THE EXPERIENCE: Open a window to your world and the feeling we get when inside.

SHOW THE VALUE: How are you different? What's the takeaway for engagement?

KANN
LEADERSHIP

MY STORY

The LPGA

How, Why and What it Meant for Me

Have you ever handed out a business card to someone, not knowing or expecting anything would come of it? What if something actually did?

That's what happened to me.

As a result of handing a business card to newly minted LPGA Commissioner Michael Whan in 2010 after I interviewed him in our Golf Channel studios as he made a stop on his introductory "media tour."

I didn't hand him a Golf Channel business card. I handed him one of my HTK Media business cards and told him that I'd love to help him on a consulting basis as he ramped things up for an organization that was in dire need of a shot in the arm.

Remember, at the time I was working four days a week at Golf Channel and had that gift of an extra day to build a side consulting business.

At the time, he thanked me and told me he'd keep it and he'd look forward to seeing me down the road. He said he would let me know if he ever needed anything.

Months later, our roads intersected.

In June of 2011, I was sitting in the Marriott hotel outside Washington, D.C., having a bite of breakfast next to commentator David Feherty when my phone rang.

"Kraig? It's Mike Whan with the LPGA."

I remember it well. About fifty feet to my right was my boss, Tom Stathakes, sitting in the lobby.

Whan said he had something in mind that I would probably dismiss very quickly. But he wanted to run it by me nonetheless.

"You'll probably tell me to go jump off a bridge," he said. That was pretty funny.

I was all ears. He said he was calling to gauge my interest in joining him as the LPGA's Chief Communications Officer with a mission of taking the organization to the next level. He said he wanted somebody who understood media, media relations, communicating a message, and who could help raise the awareness of the organization, its touring professionals, and its teaching professionals.

The way I took it was that he was looking for an 'outside the box' hire who could help him elevate brand awareness on all levels and add unique value to a great executive leadership team he was building.

His organization was in great need of added attention. He had a vision. He had ideas. He had big energy to deliver on both.

I was blown away because I never saw something like this coming. Frankly, I didn't even know the position was open – which said something about the organization's state of awareness to folks like me who were industry insiders to begin with. I didn't even know who had previously held the top communications position.

I'd always had an interest in figuring out what my "next" was going to be. Suddenly, here it might just be. Did God have a plan in the works? Time to wrestle with another big decision.

As I told the few trusted folks in my inner circle and said to myself many times during the decision process, sports executive jobs in the C-Suite don't just fall into the laps of guys like me who wore make-up and read teleprompters for a living. This was a unique development and I had to take it seriously.

Mike and I had a few private breakfast meetings where we discussed the LPGA's current state, what the job would entail, and what his vision for the organization was as a whole. My interest was piqued for many reasons. The biggest being that I would be given a chance to make a difference.

The last few years at Golf Channel had given me great cause for pause – both personally and professionally. I wasn't in love with the way some of the most loyal and talented people across the company had been treated, and while I was always incredibly proud of what Golf Channel meant for golf, I had some concerns – strong concerns – about the current and future culture. At the time, I wasn't the only one.

Helping Lead the LPGA's Brand Resurgence

There is nothing more important than how you treat people.

When you'd given your everything to take a network from ten million homes to more than one hundred and twenty-five million, never had a personal or professional misstep, and then suddenly saw loyalty kicked to the curb, health benefits pulled from your family and removed from the invitation list to the annual Christmas party because you were no longer a full-time employee, your outlook changes. It just does. Anyone who would see it differently isn't telling the truth.

I kept asking myself how I could be a primary studio host of the network, treat people the right way, deliver a professional product every day and night, and not have any commitment from them. I know I wasn't alone.

Again, and again, the question kept coming to my mind. Was I just making another television show each day, or was I making a difference?

That's what I wrestled with.

After days of processing my thoughts, hours on the phone with my tight inner circle, and hours talking about it with my wife, I came to a decision - the toughest of my career without question.

The week before the 2011 PGA Championship, I had made up my mind that I was going to take a major career turn, drop television, and become a sports executive. The thought that kept coming to me was that if it worked out great, I'd be on my way to a fulfilling "second act," and if it didn't or was something I didn't like, I could most likely get back into broadcasting at some level.

What an interesting week it turned out to be.

On the weekend before leaving for Atlanta, I'd made plans to speak with Whan at his club in Orlando to accept the job. Then I'd head to the PGA Championship, knowing it was my last big event and privately talk with Golf Channel leadership to let them know of what had been a secret for a few months.

Things got interesting.

Saturday night, I received a call from my agent at the time, Matt Kramer. Kramer was Atlanta based with CSE and he had some news for me. "The Golf Channel wants you back full time," he said. "And they want to know what your number is." Number being the salary requirement I'd be requesting in what would be a potential new contract negotiation.

We were having a party at our house with friends on the lake and it didn't take me long to respond.

"I don't have a number," I said. "I'm going to accept the position with the LPGA and I'll let them know this week, so please keep this between us for now." That's what I told Matt Kramer.

Letting Golf Channel brass know of my plans wasn't easy. I tried to do it all the right way and talk with Stathakes at Atlanta Athletic Club, but couldn't get a meeting with him coordinated that week. So, I pulled his right-hand man, Joe Riley, aside to tell him. He was surprised for sure.

Then I had a private conversation with Golf Channel President Mike McCarley on the set of *"Live From the PGA Championship."* That wasn't easy because Mike had treated me quite well. None of it was. I loved that place and gave everything of myself each and every day. To be honest, I never really had a great desire to leave.

I asked them to allow me to get through the week without telling my teammates, which I would do the next week after the major was complete. We all agreed to that.

That week, I had all of my on-air *"Live From"* co-workers sign a PGA Championship flag. Little did they know it was a personal keepsake for me.

The next week, McCarley graciously allowed me to have a final show. I hosted *Grey Goose 19th Hole* and told my co-workers of my decision to leave the Golf Channel that day in our pre-show meeting. I cried doing it.

My family came in that night to watch my final show. Just as there were tears from me in front of my teammates at the meeting, there were tears again after the show. My young girls, Hailey and Kendall, cried too. It was pretty emotional all around.

A press release about my move quickly went out from Golf Channel and also the LPGA. Just like that, the biggest career chapter of my life had ended.

I didn't take much time off. Partly the excitement from a new career opportunity and also a fear that time off might make me question my decision to leave Golf Channel.

And so, just a few weeks later, I was driving an hour from Orlando to Daytona Beach each day to a corner office instead of twenty minutes down the road to the familiar studio and a desk cubicle and a newsroom. Strange, but also exciting for sure.

My start with the LPGA was exhilarating, yet a bit personally and professionally awkward. It wasn't easy walking into an organization of people outside the television industry I'd lived in for so long.

With Commissioner Mike Whan, Lydia Ko & Inbee Park

With more than seventeen years at the Golf Channel under my belt, I had reached the degree of being a "recognized face." That's something I never took lightly, but with that also comes an inner feeling that others think that ***you*** think you're a notch above them. It's hard to explain, but it's real. I've never felt that way, or tried to be anything but a regular guy and always professional, but you can't control of how others might perceive you. You do your best to not be "the slick TV guy," but it's hard to shape an image that others form before they even know you.

Mike Whan playfully referred to me as "the talent." But I don't think it helped my transition of just trying to fit in and find my way.

I moved into a very nice office with great enthusiasm for the opportunity that I felt honored to have even been offered. Mike took me to lunch and laid out a more specific idea of his goals for the organization and me. I took notes and I still have them today. The challenge was really motivating and I was up for the strategic effort of elevating the organization, its players, and members.

It was the first time I went into a job without a clear-cut daily mission. In television, you do a show or multiple shows each day and there is a result. At day's end, the show is over and you can't change it or improve it or build on it. In sports management, you're developing a team, building on ideas, and executing plans that take time.

Whan sat in my office one day a few weeks into the job to see how I was enjoying things and said that success after leaving something I knew so well would mean "getting comfortable with the uncomfortable." That was really good advice and something I carried in my mind to battle the feeling of missing television. He gave me a lot of good advice.

My transition was unique. And if I had a dollar for every time someone asked me, "Do you miss television?" – I'd have been able to single-handedly elevate LPGA tournament purses to the level Whan was chasing!

When I got to the LPGA in 2011, there was a clear cut image problem and an awareness problem – something Whan inherited and assembled a team to help correct. The tournament schedule was down to twenty-four, the year-long prize money was just north of forty million dollars and television coverage on Golf Channel was tape-delayed on a regular basis.

LPGA Communications Team 2014

Fans weren't connected, media wasn't enthused, and players weren't truly engaged. That was the reality.

But, I'll say this, the executive leadership team and those around the building and outside headquarters were ready and willing to do their fair share.

For me, it was about assembling a fast-moving, dynamic communications team that understood how to promote, how to tell stories, and how to build real relationships with players and media.

I turned a great deal of responsibility to a sharp young guy in his late twenties named Mike Scanlan and a dedicated former baseball writer named Kelly Thesier. Others on the team, who'd seemingly just handled whatever came their way each day, now took on specific roles with new expectations to deliver.

And whenever I had the chance, I hired someone who I felt brought talents to the team what would make others have to do more just to keep up. I wanted staff members who would push others – and me – to do their job better. And when it made sense, I made it my goal to hire the best woman at every opportunity. I felt I owed that to the LPGA, which was all about opportunities for women.

My first hire was a young woman named Meghan Flanagan, who was organized and energetic beyond words. She showed up for her interview with a portfolio of her work while at Rutgers and a message that she was there to make a difference and not waste anyone's time. She had confidence. She had spunk. She was an easy choice.

In five years, with names like Ali Kicklighter, Bret Lasky, Molly Gallatin, Nick Parker, Tina Budd, and Matt Haas, we built a uber-talented team who understood the meaning of "relations" at every turn. Media **relations**, player **relations**, community and tournament **relations**, and sponsor **relations.**

I pushed a few things during my time. One was a "beat system" for media and tournaments – just like a media member would have in dealing with the police beat or the political beat or the educational beat. Each team member was responsible for a handful of media members and a small group of tournaments they would work hard to deliver our information and our stories.

Another thing I put into place was a "player communications committee." Each year, I asked eight players to join me on a committee where we would work together to create ideas that would garner attention for the organization and build plans to execute them. I also told them I'd share everything I could about where the commissioner was headed and what we were planning, provided they came with ideas that could supplement that. And lastly, before agreeing to come on board, I asked that each player look in the mirror and see the entire organization and not just themselves – meaning that we were all pulling toward the bigger goal.

Having a laugh with Suzann Pettersen

More than forty players took part over five years, and only one person took a pass on the opportunity. I asked American players, international players, veterans, younger players, and moms as well. I wanted the whole snapshot of who the LPGA was each week so that everyone had a voice.

Michelle Wie, Stacy Lewis, Inbee Park, Yani Tseng, Morgan Pressel, Paige McKenzie, Anna Nordqvist, So Young Ryu, Brittany Lincicome, Nicole Castrale, Shanshan Feng, Jessica Korda, Sandra Gal, and Pernilla Lindberg were among those who not only agreed to take part, but made big contributions in presenting their ideas that would help us gain media attention.

People ask me which player impressed me the most during my time. And that is an easy answer.

I was brand new to the organization in 2011, and the first event I went to was a stop in Montreal for the Canadian Women's Open. I walked into the hotel as an LPGA "rookie," and the first player to greet me with a welcome was Norwegian superstar Suzann Pettersen. People saw her as the tough, laser-focused, veteran who wasn't the most welcoming and was one of the most volatile on the course because she was so competitive. Some of that was true and I had obviously covered her and delivered "Pettersen highlights" while on the set of *Golf Central.*

From the moment of "hello," I saw a player who was open and friendly. People said she was stiff and uninterested. They said she never smiled either. So, with that, I jokingly called her "Smiley" every time I saw her. It stuck and she embraced it.

Pettersen never joined my communications committee, but I never asked. She gave me plenty of her time and many unsolicited thoughts about how the LPGA could grow. She cared more than anyone would truly know. She became a confidant and trusted friend. And she appreciated my interest in coming into the job with a purpose and a passion. So much so, that she asked me to fly to Oslo and emcee her big hometown charity event. I took her up on it, and the next year when I had a family conflict, she flew my wife over with me to make things work out. I've never forgotten that.

During my time at the LPGA, I traveled more than I expected, but I always tried to do it with a plan and a purpose. My team and I focused on making media feel welcome and appreciated in every community and worked to make sure that our players over delivered on media expectations. I presented media coaching seminars at night for large groups of players, with the concept being "opportunity over obligation." I shared strategic ways they could create and better share their story.

2013 Solheim Cup with Lizette Salas and Stacy Lewis

My relationship with Golf Channel was key because we were able to willingly put our athletes on shows that PGA TOUR pros didn't have time for. And I pushed hard for every opportunity we could get, be it television or radio or print outlets. Our communications team was relentless in creating relationships and together, we created powerful and dynamic press conferences to deliver our news that were not what people had been used to.

We tried to be different.

I remember when Japanese carrier All Nippon Airways took over as the sponsor for the year's first major in Rancho Mirage, California. ANA was looking for a brand presence in the United States and we were determined to deliver. When they were announced, not only did we put ANA executives on the stage with Commissioner Whan, but we brought in a group of flight attendants who would escort people to their seats and work the stage during the press conference. The announcement included a video of the commissioner in an airplane making a statement. It was visually different and it got people talking.

After the press conference, a key member of the media came up to me and said, "Kraig, you don't do press conferences, you do productions!" That meant a lot and it was something I preached to our team.

"Let's not do things because they've always been done that way before," I said. "Let's do them a different way because nobody's tried." In other words, don't follow the curve; let's find a way to set the curve.

In addition to traveling to tournaments, I hosted press conferences and gave speeches when the commissioner wasn't able. I was given the opportunity to produce and emcee our biggest events. And I was charged with delivering media and awareness for global sponsors who'd come on board. From Kuala Lumpur, Malaysia to Evian, France to Seoul, Korea to Honolulu, Hawaii, and points all across the United States, I spoke at press conferences, sponsor events, and tournament galas, and I loved it. It was about building the image of the LPGA and getting people engaged.

Broadcasting the LPGA story was a terrific opportunity. I loved the product and I lived it in my work - out in front of people - as best I knew how. Privately, I called myself a "passion promoter."

In addition to my role inside the organization, I represented the LPGA on industry committees leading communication efforts and messaging for the game of golf and the organizations that drove the sport.

Nothing felt bigger than a role with the International Golf Federation and the 2016 Rio Olympic Games. Bringing golf back to the Olympics after more than a century was no small order. The PGA TOUR and LPGA were asked to deliver players and messages to raise attention and show the International Olympic Committee that they'd made the right choice in picking golf over other sports for a spot on the roster.

For more than two years of my five-year stint with the LPGA, we worked on overdrive to build momentum for the Olympics. While the PGA TOUR was having trouble convincing players that a trip to Brazil was a safe proposition because of the Zika virus spread by mosquitoes, the LPGA players were far more open to the global stage awaiting women's golf. None of us were surprised. As I said many times, the LPGA players simply get it.

With all the great things going on with the LPGA, sometimes, even the best career opportunities get tangled up with personal struggle. I know I'm not alone when it comes to that reality.

Three-plus years into my run as the LPGA's Chief Communications Officer, I was in a tough spot on the home front and staring at the unthinkable – divorce. Years of drifting apart took a toll. While completely enjoying my time at the LPGA, and respecting the role and responsibility I had, the daily drive from Orlando to Daytona Beach mixed with the frequent airplane flights and challenges to keep things right in my marriage was mentally wearing me out.

The divorce process began early in 2015, after almost twenty-four years. Inside, my body was a wreck. It was tough on the family for sure. My door at work was often closed. I was struggling. Being in an executive role, I think you try to hold yourself to a high standard and not let people see your flaws or your struggles. I tried to hide it all. I didn't do it well.

Among the things I learned was that while you think immersing yourself into your work as a solution to coping with a life-altering personal challenge, it's tough to do. I was trying to keep it all together and manage a team and stand in front of audiences - and it wasn't easy.

I specifically remember two of my speaking engagements that went poorly because I was an emotional basket case. One was in front of the entire group of players at a huge meeting and the other was in Detroit at a sponsor event. One was obvious and the other was probably not as apparent. Strangely enough, those two talks have helped me greatly because I have learned – now – how to calm myself when I feel like anxiety is at a higher level.

Emcee at LPGA's Rolex Gala
Naples, FL

The other thing pulling at me was the possibility that I could take my true passion for speaking and leading and media coaching and make it into a full-time business.

I had a couple of career coaches who emphasized that I'd spent a lot of time investing in building my brand and that I shouldn't apologize for that. Maybe now, they said, was the time to use the years of experience and put them to use for others, and make an impact helping companies, their leaders, and even athletic organizations to deliver a bigger message and present themselves in the best possible way to create impact.

One night in Naples, at the LPGA's year-end awards gala, a woman in attendance, who I respected and admired for her efforts in the industry, basically cemented that thought in my mind. I had a speech presentation and presented an award that night. While walking off the stage back to my seat, she pulled me aside and said, "Kraig, you need to be speaking to bigger audiences and doing something even bigger."

It stopped me in my tracks. It meant a lot, especially from her. And she said it at the right time.

USA TODAY SPORTS

All eyes on France

The European Championship kicks off Friday in France, on alert for terrorism but still standing tall as a symbol of peace, unity, 10C

Taking pages from peers' playbooks

Sharing info with other college coaches during offseason has benefits, risks

Paul Myerberg

Temple's Matt Rhule, right, with Brian Kelly, has met with Virginia Tech's Justin Fuente and Air Force's Troy Calhoun.

STORY CONTINUES ON 10C

IT'S TIME TO PAY ATTENTION TO LPGA TOUR

Women's golf has plenty of appeal

Christine Brennan

USA TODAY Sports

SAMMAMISH, WASH. One by one they come to the media center at the KPMG Women's PGA Championship to tell their stories of sports success, athletes most of us don't know, but certainly should.

Tell me, sports fans, do you know the name Lydia Ko? She has been the No. 1-ranked player in the world in women's golf for 83 consecutive weeks. Golf fans must know her. But the casual sports fan?

How about Lexi Thompson? She could win the Olympic gold medal for the United States in women's golf in Rio in two months. Please tell me you've heard of her.

Ariya Jutanugarn? Stacy Lewis? Inbee Park?

How about Nancy Lopez?

That was a trick question. Of course you've heard of Nancy Lopez.

The USA's Lexi Thompson has seven career LPGA tour wins and is ranked No. 8 in the world.

LPGA pullout

USA Today – June, 2016

In my years at the LPGA, I felt like I was a pretty good boss. I delegated key opportunities and focused my attention on building stars in our department worthy of internal promotion or even recruitment by other organizations. I wanted people on my team who could also stand before groups and deliver for the organization and build excitement for our events and promote our members. We did that together. Everyone on the team brought a specific expertise or value. My communications team was amazing.

In a five-year run of many highlights, two stand out.

The first happened In 2015. We received a letter from Sports Business Journal that the LPGA had been named one of five finalists for "Sports League of the Year." To our knowledge, that had never happened.

It was validation for many things; Whan's vision that led the organization on a path from twenty-four tournaments to thirty-three with more hours of live television than at any time in the LPGA's history. A rise in year-long prize money from forty-plus million to over sixty and an overall shift in culture that had sponsors, fans, stakeholders, and players alike feeling like the LPGA was indeed relevant and respected.

A handful of us flew to New York City for the biggest awards night in sports business. So cool to be among every big-name executive in sports and sports media, including some of the biggest broadcast voices in sports.

While we didn't win the top honor, I actually make it a point to tell everyone that we did, in fact, win. We won by inclusion. Because we showed the power of influence and togetherness from all circles of the organization, we proved we were worthy of being showcased. We had also proven there is great power in positive media. Attention to the organization seemed to be at an all-time high.

The second highlight for me came near the end of my tenure in 2016.

My final two big events were the Olympic Games in Rio that August and the Evian Championship in France a month later.

In Rio, my role was to host the Olympic press conferences for women's golf. It was a thrill. Sitting there with some of the world's best female athletes, moderating their moment of lifetime achievement was so rewarding.

An Emotional Farewell with Lydia Ko in Evian, France

But the most emotional moment came on the stage at the Evian Championship – a major on the LPGA schedule.

I was the evening's master of ceremonies at the Rolex Awards night, which honored the winners of the year's major championships and the Rolex Annika Major Award winner. It was my last event before I left to go full throttle into my new business venture.

And I never expected what was about to happen that night.

In the midst of an interview with the year's top major performers, LPGA superstar Lydia Ko grabbed the mic from me and brought me to a flood of emotions in front of a packed house. She shared with folks that I was leaving the organization and talked about the impact she believed I had made and the passion and energy she saw me give. I was touched, nearly to tears, on that stage. And I will forever remember that as a sign of my efforts. Working with Lydia, and others like Inbee Park and Michelle Wie and Suzann Pettersen and Brittany Lincicome and Stacy Lewis was an honor because they made it so. It was their organization – not mine – and they deserved everyone's best efforts.

What people don't know about the LPGA, unless they've lived it, is that every member – be it player or teaching professional – and every sponsor or partner or employee has pride in women's golf and an organization that dedicates itself to finding a real voice. It's powerful. And I was glad to have used my voice to help make a difference.

Why did I sign up in 2011? Because I thought I could do something equally or more important than I had done while being a voice and face of golf on television. I wanted to learn to be an executive and I wanted to help athletes who deserved better in terms of recognition and compensation. It was the most challenging five years of my career and probably the most rewarding.

Why did I leave? That's complicated. If you can thread together the conflicting world of feeling like you'd reached the goals set before you, feeling uncertainty about what would be left to accomplish or what else could or would be put before you that gave you the right energy, then you have half of it. Add in the tug to put your name on your own business while the time felt right and before it might be too late to try, then you've got it.

My personal life situation hadn't helped me, either. Two hours a day in the car back and forth to the office, coupled with hours and hours on airplanes, had taken a toll on personal balance. And when things go wrong there, it's tough to stay focused.

LPGA Executives at SBJ Awards Night in New York, NY

As I've admitted, I've always struggled with the status quo and felt like I wanted to be there more for my family. And what nobody knew was that I was struggling personally with the present and what would happen in the future.

My friend Jeff Rude is more than just a well-respected journalist. He's a deep thinker with great perspective I've used in many ways. He's often repeated that sometimes life jumbles far too many things in our head and we tend to try to control things we can't control. In that case, he says we need to be patient and "let the universe sort out the details for us." In this case, the details sorted themselves out.

It was time to put my name and my passion on something new.

CHAPTER FIFTEEN

My Career Thoughts To Win

From My Experience to YOU

You can work with the goal of being comfortable, or you can work with the goal of being outstanding. It's your choice.

Time for me to share some big picture career thoughts – perhaps it will help you define or redefine some goals or perhaps reflect on your own success. By no means do I know it all, but as the Farmers Insurance ad says, "I know a thing or two because I've seen a thing or two."

In 2008 when the economic market changed, so too did my outlook on business and career. It absolutely altered the lens from which I viewed my present and future employment.

I was comfortably entrenched at Golf Channel/NBC as a host and anchor. I'd worked hard to get there - the result of 20 years of experience in various local television markets. And the excitement of building the brand of golf's biggest television enterprise had been extremely satisfying.

Still, the television industry was changing. Cable networks were popping up everywhere, mergers were taking place, and escalating rights fees for live sporting events dominated headlines. Transition in the industry meant cuts and once secure contracts for "talent" were left open for debate from executives who may or may not have been long for their own positions.

With uncertainty for many, I became more certain than ever.

I knew that I needed to widen my platform and find a way to broaden my skill set. Being known for only one thing (television host) might not put me in the best position moving forward. That was my thought, anyway.

So, I started planning for a future that could include something new. That meant developing me. It meant digging deep into who I was and what I wanted for me in the long term.

Here are three principles I have always lived by that came to the forefront of my mind as I went back in time to get a clearer picture of where I was headed.

- **Believe that success or failure can happen before you even make the effort** – It's all about your mindset and mine was clear. It was time to focus a little more on preparing myself for what could or might be next rather than what was now. That meant self-assessment and thinking about what I'd learned and what I could share that would present me as a valued expert.

  I think a lot of people just plod along in a career doing what they do and don't think about a goal of being special and unique at what they do. In other words, they get too comfortable.
- **Always work to make a difference and not a paycheck** – A former boss once suggested that we should focus on opportunities when we are young and leave the later years of our career to make money count. Sound advice. I listened.

  I spent a lot of my early career with a mindset of grabbing any and every bit of experience I could get. Let's face it, when you're barely making twenty thousand dollars a year as a young sportscaster, having a narrowed mindset with money as a main source of happiness would only send you spiraling into bouts of depression. With what I was making, I couldn't afford the counseling sessions anyway!

  Along my path, the idea of chasing opportunities for growth became even bigger. And that would be my message to anyone. Money is what I call "value validation." Opportunities that inspire hold great value too. So, don't stop growing your personal talent toolbox. You'll probably need it at some point and the more you can offer, the more opportunities you'll find around the corner.
- **Always challenge yourself to overdeliver on expectations** – Take what's put in front of you and deliver something in return that's more than anyone expected. Whether it was the second of three shows in a single day at Golf Channel, the next big press conference at the LPGA, or the upcoming speaking appearance or corporate workshop, I've privately tried to one-up myself.

  Going through the motions at work becomes quite transparent. Trust me, everyone sees it. It becomes your brand. People know when you just "complete projects." It's when you deliver extraordinary over ordinary that people take notice

Whether it was the second show of three in a day at Golf Channel, or the next big press conference at the LPGA, or the most recent speaking appearance or corporate workshop, I have always tried to one-up myself. Shouldn't we all try to do better the next time?

Going through the motions at work becomes quite transparent. Trust me, everyone sees it. It becomes your brand. People know when you just "complete projects." It's when you deliver something that stands out that people take notice.

Success is based on the right opportunities. Making them happen should be what drives you.

Shouldn't we all strive to do things that make people take notice? Opportunities don't come around all that often. Great ones rarely do. But when they do, we need to overdeliver and show people that we're worthy of the chance to show something special.

Think about what people are saying about the things you are doing – or not doing. It's a powerful motivator and something that will serve you well no matter what age.

I received a phone call recently that stood out for me. A member of the media and a respected member of the PGA of America – golf's most recognized organization for teaching and club professionals – called me to help a friend of his with public speaking.

The man who called made it clear that I had been top of mind when it came to helping people become better in front of an audience. He said he'd been watching my content on social media and following my new professional journey closely. I appreciated that very much, but what struck me during the call was just how things had evolved for me. Over the years, the very same person had made comments appreciating me for my efforts as a broadcaster. Now, he was praising me for something else.

My point in sharing is that my decision to shift my career, not being afraid to put myself out there, showcasing a new skillset, had paid off in terms of what is possible. And what people may see you for! Go back up to the first thing I mentioned a few paragraphs ago. I said, "success or failure can happen before you even make the effort. It's all about your mindset."

The message is that you aren't stuck in cement shoes when it comes to your career. I'm proof that you don't have to remain in the same line of work. What happens from here is all about how determined you are to set sail and how well you can marry your years of experience. Everyone can take what they have done, figure out how it helped, and then put it toward helping others – all while making something new of yourself.

If you want to win with your story, think wider about your career. Don't be afraid to change. It's not a new brand that awaits you. It can be a "brand new you" that has expanded and grown.

KRAIG'S LIST

3 THINGS: Why Goals Matter So Much

PURPOSE: Gives us a much needed life vision and reason to push.

PURSUIT: Career clarity helps keep us on track. What are we pushing for exactly?

PAYOFF: What's your pot at the rainbow's end? Know your definition of "arrived."

KANN LEADERSHIP

CHAPTER SIXTEEN

My Career Thoughts To Win

Get Comfortable Being an Uncomfortable YOU

The more solid bricks in your career foundation, the more you have to offer to others. Spread your professional wings and keep growing.

Have you ever sat down, put pen to paper or fingers to a computer keyboard, and laid out your career trail?

I'm not just talking about the companies or organizations you worked for. It's more than that. I'm talking about the cities you called home, the people you met at various jobs, and the people you came to know because of the opportunities you had and the experiences that stand out.

When we share our story, it all becomes a part of the special narrative unique to each of us.

Our brand is built with blocks that form a foundation of who we are. And thus, what we can offer to others as we continue forward.

Sometimes, we take a role, accept our title, and move forward with a tunnel vision of exactly what is expected from us. We use our skillset to deliver on the expectation and we stay right in our lane.

While focusing on being the best I could in every given role, I admit to being a person who has always been looking around to see what else I could add to my resume.

While at the Golf Channel, I was always hesitant when contract negotiation time rolled around. I would be offered a new agreement for one, two, or in some cases, four years. While more than appreciative, a part of me was nervous because while I was loyal and wanted no part of leaving, I wanted to know what I was signing up for. What show or shows would I host? What new challenge might there be in addition to what I was already doing? How much travel was I in line for? Things like that came to mind.

In today's world, two years is a long time to do the same thing. Four years seems like an eternity.

I wasn't always looking for a promotion. I was finding new ways to improve and challenge myself. But I was also looking to expand my roles and opportunities. Some of which I was more than ready for. And in asking for additional opportunities, I might have actually been putting myself in a box outside my comfort zone. That's okay. I wanted to stretch myself.

Think about all the things you have done in your career.

If your story is centered on one place of employment, ask yourself just how exciting it is to share it when telling your story.

If you've held the same title for more than five years or maybe ten, is there enough personal or professional growth in that for you?

I think the answers come pretty quickly.

Wouldn't a great goal be to find new avenues for growth within our current role structure?

And if we want to take our game to the next level, then don't we need to find opportunities that place us in front of new challenges and new audiences?

Keep in mind; I'm not telling you to look for a new job. Hardly the case. I'm suggesting you look to build a new and better you within the one you have.

I'm pretty confident that my skills as a broadcaster allowed me to succeed in certain opportunities communicating the LPGA message. I'm also fairly confident that my role in the media asking questions gave me the credibility to become a good media coach with LPGA players or executives looking for an edge in delivering their story. And I'm pretty certain speaking in front of sponsors and corporate groups in both roles allowed me to be quite comfortable in a workshop or on a stage sharing the finer points of presentation skills to corporate teams, marketing groups, or sales leaders.

One thing helps another thing which helps another.

Sit down and figure out what your top professional skills might be and where your greatest skills have been built.

Now, *what else* can you do with them?

Transferable skills make you valuable. They allow you to become attractive to organizations outside your own. Don't ever stop finding new areas of knowledge and new opportunities to tackle. And wherever possible, look hard for ways to put yourself in what I like to call "areas of the uncomfortable."

The tougher the challenge, the more you have to think and prepare, and the more you learn about yourself.

As I have said, I had no idea if I could be a successful chief communications officer or a valuable member of an executive leadership team. But in going through the steps of learning about the role and also myself, I found my way to being *me* in that role. Some would say I was good at it. Some would say I wasn't as good as I could have been.

To be honest, I'm okay with the opinions on both sides. And you should be too. It's okay to fall short of other's definition of perfection. Our goal is to climb and stretch ourselves. Our goal should be to be the best that we can be. I hope they'll say that I gave great effort to be my best and that I was different.

So many people say they want more opportunities, but how many people truly do something with the ones they get? Be that person.

How many people have you heard complain about not being given more opportunities? Probably a pretty big number. Everyone seems to want the promotion. But how many people are actually willing to show their boss that they want more work or responsibility – even if it's something they don't have years of experience doing?

Be the person who isn't afraid to ask for more.

Also, be the person who has shown the ability to excel at what's already been given.

Find your way to being recognized among a small group of people that stands out in a crowd.

Be the person whose foundation of career-building blocks has a few visible cracks as proof that not everything has come easy.

And show them you're okay with failing because you took on something they didn't think you would.

Nobody's foundation is smooth. Gosh knows I've certainly failed. I've had some pretty bad shows, some bad speeches, and a few meetings where I could have been better with my teammates.

Nobody has navigated the ocean without a few troubled waters. That's what gives us experience and calm to perform better when the next challenge or opportunity comes our way.

If you want to win with your story, spread your wings whenever possible. Start getting comfortable with things that are uncomfortable.

Your results will surprise you. The stories others will tell about you, and your story becomes a whole lot more interesting.

KRAIG'S LIST

3 THINGS: My Take on Opportunity

NOT GIVEN: Earned. Some never get tapped. Why YOU?

NOT GUARANTEED: Potentially taken away if we don't over-deliver.

NOT FOR GRANTED: Complacency's a killer. Success with any chance leads to more.

KANN LEADERSHIP

MY STORY

The Kann Advisory Group

A New Brand & The Inspiration to Build It

It's funny how brands begin and how companies take shape. I think it all comes down to two things; an idea and the passion to go along with it.

As I mentioned earlier, while at Golf Channel in 2009, I had an extra day during the week to do something outside of television. And HTK Media was born. *"Hire the Knowledge, Have the Knowledge"* was the message behind the business, which gave me an opportunity to consult with companies and individuals, conduct workshops on presentation skills and media coach corporate folks and athletes and coaches. It also gave me a positive distraction from television, a new challenge, and a chance to build something that was uniquely mine.

I remember when the HTK Media website was complete. A few weeks with a small company in Orlando that made a vision come to life. Simple, colorful, informative, and mine. It was a proud moment.

In just a couple of years, working only a few days a month, I had started building something I was proud of and something that provided a service that gave value to others. The business earned some money, and the testimonials shared by happy customers probably helped me with more than just the next client.

Just doing it helped me land the opportunity with the LPGA in 2011 as I had more than just experience broadcasting and presenting golf. I was helping corporations and organizations present themselves better. And I was empowering people to think bigger and present better. As a mission, I was working to help people become their professional best.

In my conversations with Mike Whan prior to joining the LPGA, I was pretty clear that HTK Media was something I didn't want to just toss aside. I was "all in" on being a part of his leadership team but we came to an agreement that if something came up involving media or a consulting or speaking opportunity and it didn't affect my work schedule or take my focus away from my main thing, I would present it to Mike and we'd try to make it work. He was great about it.

Yet optically, it was all more difficult than I expected.

I had already built a website that had been running for a couple of years and established a social media presence with the HTK Media brand. In addition, I was blogging regularly on a site with promotional material tied to the small company I had built. Despite the fact that my content included

LPGA on many occasions, it must have rubbed a few people the wrong way or at least caused some confusion about whether I was truly full-time with the LPGA or perhaps spreading myself across two professional platforms.

Hardly the case. My job was with the LPGA and it was more than a full-time responsibility. And it was one I took very seriously. But I understood how perception might have felt different.

Here's what I can tell you about having a business of any kind. If you have it, you have to tell people you have it. Nobody just figures it out on their own. Our agreement to allow me that "side business" was never really sustainable, or at least never really carried out, as we discussed in our original conversations. So, for the time being, the concept behind HTK Media was slowed in a big way.

At the beginning of 2016, more than four years into my role with the LPGA, I remember setting my goals for the year as we continued on a growth path and greater attention for the organization and its members. For the first time since I had joined in 2011, I struggled to develop a new set of achievable goals that took us where we hadn't been before. Finding something new and exciting within the confines of the budget was a challenge. And my mind started wandering a bit, thinking about what the future would look like if I stayed on long term.

The future became the present in October of 2016, just a few weeks after leaving the LPGA.

I had been meeting with a career coach for a few months and was leaning on a few friends who were successfully entrenched with the company or running their own small business. And each of them strongly suggested the same thing.

They all said I needed to use my name and re-brand the company.

Anyone reading this would probably agree that putting your name out there as a brand is a bit uncomfortable. And it was. But the logic behind it was that I had a real value offering to share and I would be foolish to not use the name credibility I had worked so hard to establish.

And so it was, HTK Media became Kann Advisory Group.

I added "Group" because of my rolodex and long list of connections. If I was going to get into the consulting business, travel to companies and organizations sharing knowledge and helping them, why not bring someone along who could provide added value? If it was media coaching, why not bring an athlete or sports broadcaster or somebody who'd worked as a media director for a professional sports league or team? If it was a workshop on leadership or presentation skills, could I add another established talent in the same arena? And if it all became really big, "Group" allowed me to grow in adding partners. I wanted a company name that was identifiable, simple, and reflective of what I was doing.

Two things had to happen quickly.

I needed a logo with a good slogan or tagline. And I needed a website.

As far as the company slogan, Nike has "Just Do It." Apple has "Think Different." Mine came without too much stress.

I had always liked the idea of "elevating" others and helping people, organizations, and events to go to the next level. It was something we talked a lot about at the LPGA – elevating the members, the tournaments, and the organization as a whole. And the concept of "elevate" gave me the fit with what I felt I brought to anything I had done in my career. Every day, whether in television or sports business, I was committed to elevating the product and the people around me.

My tagline became *"Elevating Communication,"* and it fit perfectly with the logo concept I had drawn up in my head and also on paper.

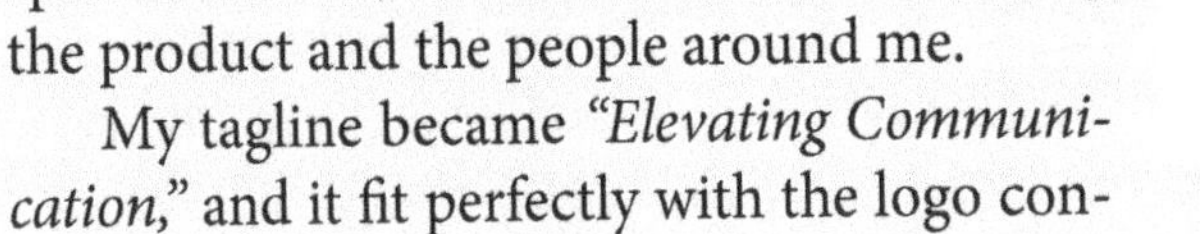

Putting pen to paper was the start. And it didn't take long to see that the "A" in KANN could be the mountain that would serve as the over-all image for the business. A mountain peak that screamed, "elevate."

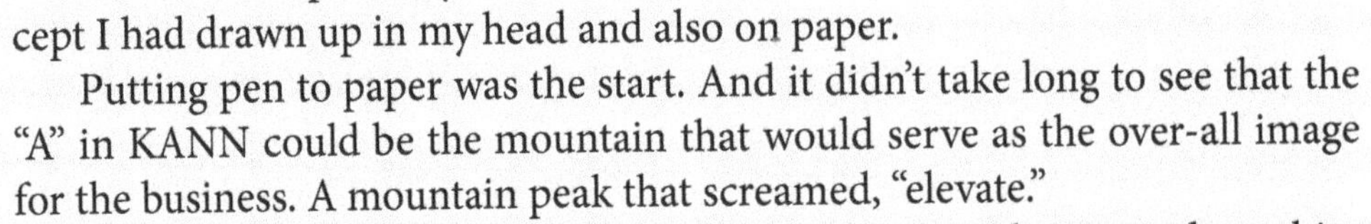

I drew up a couple of models and called a local marketing and graphics design company to meet and create mock-ups. I also sent it to my brother, Brian, who has developed a few logos of his own and has a pretty good eye for stuff like this. His logo was pretty close to the final result. I sent his drawing to the team I was working with, and before I knew it, I had the logo for my re-branded business.

Next came the website. It was more time consuming than I had imagined describing my offerings and coming up with images. My first website was off an online platform and it got me going. It's not the one I use today, but it was a smart start.

Keeping your messaging clear and simple is a challenge. I enjoyed it.

All along, I have been fortunate to have people who believed in what I was doing and who encouraged me to simply go for it. One of those people was Jon Newsome, who leads an Atlanta-based company called Presentation Partners. Jon has ties to golf, knew of me from my days on-air at Golf Channel. In my research, I found him and was thankful he understood what I was promoting, remembered who I was, and offered to help me.

Presentation Partners is a company all about visual storytelling – basically designing slides and power points for organizations and leaders who, too often, stand before people with far too many words and ineffective images on the screen behind them. Jon's team of designers has a knack for bringing power points and business marketing collateral to life. That's what he's done for me.

I launched the re-brand and established Kann Advisory Group in November of 2016, and I was off to the races, having just ONE speaking engagement in my back pocket and a library of contacts I'd made over the years.

It wasn't much, but as I have told anyone and everyone who would listen – or who has designs on jumping head first into something like this yourself – you can't wait for everything to be perfect or you'll never get started. It was time to let passion and persistence steer me.

Here's what I haven't told anyone.

As I was launching Kann Advisory Group, I was also in contact with multiple search firm executives and I poured through industry websites with media and executive job opportunities posted.

Why?

My philosophy was that I needed a back-up plan in case momentum took longer than I could afford. Perhaps my smartest move was that I used every phone call to every contact as a "research project" to learn about potential opportunities within the market that might be a potential fit for Kann Advisory. I used that time on the phone to find out what companies and their executives were looking for to create growth within their organizations. This proved to be very helpful.

SAP Keynote in Phoenix, AZ

I've never been one to sell a product without listening first. And the first person I listened to in the entire process of the "Kann Advisory Group build" was me. I listened to my gut. It told me to go for it with no regret. As they say, your gut is usually correct.

The first opportunities came before the end of 2016, although they wouldn't take place until January of 2017. Each was with someone I knew and had formed a relationship with over the years. To anyone starting a business, that's where I would advise you to begin.

Golf Channel had taken over the World Long Drive Association and its events and wanted to start personalizing and branding its competitors. That called for some media coaching and presentation skills training as a way of pushing out their stories. Bingo! Opportunity number one came my way and I was brought in to lead a two-day seminar as a part of Kann Advisory Group.

The second big break came from my childhood friend, Dave Hutchison, who, at the time, led SAP's national marketing branch and was looking for keynote speakers to fill out his 2017 marketing kick-off event in Phoenix. He trusted I could share a great message, and that I could also provide a series of break-out sessions on the topic of branding, executive presence, and presentation skills. I was more than ready.

Each was a home run day for me and the feedback told me I was on the right track. Soon after, I closed a one-day experience with KPMG's communication leaders based on a relationship I'd formed with its then head of communications during my years at the LPGA.

Momentum built and with each opportunity came the chance at another stage and another chance to refine and build out what would become my speaking platform and workshop experience. Most importantly, with each of the early clients came another positive testimonial that I could use as a selling point for others.

To this day, I am beyond grateful for those early events. And to the people who gave me a chance.

My business remains centered on its earliest foundation blocks that I have shared up above. It is probably no different from a few interviews or shows that got me on track at the Golf Channel and some big meetings, press conferences, or speaking opportunities that got me comfortable in my role at the LPGA.

We all can point to critical moments or events along our path that stand out as definers of our brand. Our greatest success often comes in the face of uncertainty. That's a powerful achievement. I had leaned in to uncertainty and come out on the other side.

Kann Advisory Group was off and running.

Exhibiting for Kann Advisory in Atlanta, GA

CHAPTER SEVENTEEN

A No Fear Mindset To Win

Building a Brand New YOU

Don't ever brag about what you are GOING to do. Just do it and let the merits of what you have done speak for you.

Anyone who has taken on the role of entrepreneur understands full well that you are your own head of business development, marketing, communications, sales, and everything else that goes with launching and growing your own business.

For me, it has come with a great professional and personal challenge, which I love. While I admit to having nerves, frequent bouts of anxiety, and wondering what's next or when it will come, I'm not afraid. Sometimes the opportunity of what could be is greater than the fear of what might not.

Some have thought that with the launch of my own business came a new singular focus and never again thought about returning to the world of working for someone else.

To this day, I think some don't know whether to view me as a "tv guy" or a "business executive." My thought process is simple. I commit to what I'm doing. But with it, my eyes and ears are wide open, knowing that the "next big thing" might be right around the corner. Whether it might be staying the course and working for myself or shifting again and working for someone else, I don't know.

In launching my business brand, I had to tell myself over and over not to spread the word about all I was going to do. I don't know that it sounds too good. I just sat at my desk and put thoughts to paper and words to presentations and laid out concepts that would become social media posts. I just buried myself in ideas and trying to lay them out.

I needed opportunities to go show what I could do. And I worked the phones and my network of contacts hard.

I received some great advice along the way. The first piece is one that I've already mentioned. So here it is again.

- **Treat every phone conversation or meeting with a prospective client as a research project and not a hard sell**—This has kept me focused on the person on the other end of the conversation. Their world comes first. Their pain points, their needs. That way, you can see if there is a realistic fit for doing business.

  If business doesn't come from the conversation, you gain valuable information to help shape your offerings.

  It's the same in any conversation with those you trust. Don't be afraid to ask others where your strengths are. As well, ask about things you can improve on. It becomes quite valuable as you move along and figure out what your "what" really is.
- **Keep the main thing the main thing**—As I have said in this book, I've been labeled an "ideas guy." At times, it can get the best of me because the excitement of new ideas that pop into my head can steer me away from my focus. I tend, at times, to put too many balls in the air. But I do think being an idea generator is a strength for me and I love listening to the ideas put forth by others.

  Only when you figure out your greatest strengths or offerings can you focus on making them go from good to great. The same goes for ideas. Pick the good ones and focus on getting those across the finish line.

"Always trust your gut. Chances are pretty good it's smarter than you."

As you know, my gut told me the time had come to become my own boss and share my experiences for the benefit of others – using the strength of my presentation background to present my offering in a way that many others might not be able to.

Was I nervous? Of course. Was I fearful things might not work out and I wouldn't make enough money to cover my needs and support my family? Absolutely a fact.

Remember, all at once, I was leaving the corporate world, going through a divorce and trying to figure out where my story was going to go next.

But I had put my own back against my own wall. Only then did I truly begin to really learn about myself.

My point in sharing all this? It's simple. I don't think my story is much different from that of many other folks as they progress in their careers and lives.

Things get complicated.

Fear can serve as a paralyzer or a motivator. Are you fearful that you might someday find yourself out of a job? Are you fearful that you might not get that promotion you are seeking? Are you fearful you might not have the wide range of skills you need to become a valuable commodity to the open market? Are you fearful that in your next job you might not like it? Are you fearful that in starting a business it might just fail?

I would tell you and everyone else the same thing. Don't get comfortable. Force yourself to grow and challenge your own status quo.

Owning a diverse range of experiences is helpful to everyone you come across in business. Put some money down and send yourself to a workshop or a conference and invest time in learning new things. Pour yourself into reading books that interest you on topics you don't know enough about or might want to put into action.

Network.

I believe we become better equipped to succeed by learning from others who have already done what we are hoping to do. And we also learn a lot from people who are going through it – perhaps blogging or posting about their real-life journey and the pitfalls that might accompany the triumphs.

Here are a few other things I've put into play. Thoughts I carry with me that I think can help you steer clear of fear and create a mindset for present and future successes.

- **Work to be knowable, not known**—Are you out for a raise, or are you out to raise your level of expertise? There is a difference.
- **Work to stand for something**—Make sure people know who you are, what your values are and that your effort provides important value to others.
- **Work to stand out by offering what isn't being offered**—Common doesn't really make the community a better place. Do what others don't or won't and be good at it.

Long before working on this book, I put a lot of effort into a blog and social media posts. I still do. I don't tweet or blog to be more well known. I tweet information I hope can help people or provide some real-world knowledge that others can relate to or use to their benefit in the near future. I blog to tell stories and share insight - like what people look for in a presenter, how to handle the toughest question in an interview, or how to make the close of your next speech the most engaging you've ever had.

If that information adds to my following, then great. If it gives my followers more reason to stick around, then that's a victory too. Even bigger, is a loyal band of followers who consider my posts "share worthy." The main thing is to stay focused on what makes you, you. Try to deliver bigger things and more of them in a way that's engaging. Stay committed, avoid fear, and just go for it!

I've been an employee for others. Now I'm an employee accountable to myself. Maybe that changes again, maybe not. But I know this for sure. The moment I took control of my future in my own head, thinking about how I delivered and the way I delivered, was the day I became better for the people I worked for and worked with.

I challenged myself to stand out and be more than just another employee. I didn't want to just complete tasks and do shows and return emails and hold meetings. I wanted to connect with people, enhance their experience, put the best product forward and raise awareness for it.

In doing that, I realized that the best way I could make an impact was to use my skills and build out ways to put them in front of people. And I think that's how you should look at your own professional brand. Who are you? What are your differentiators? How can they help?

Don't be afraid to reach the potential you might not have seen in yourself until you've taken the time to take a closer look. If you want to win with your story, have an entrepreneurial mindset each day. Be a champion of your ideas. And most of all, adopt a no-fear approach to seeing them cross the finish line.

Sharing with Leadership at the Missouri Lottery

KRAIG'S LIST

3 THINGS: To Build Your Winning Mindset

BRAGGING RIGHTS: Don't tell 'em what you want to do. Show 'em what you've done.

NO LANE CHANGE: Keep your main thing your main thing. Focus is a great skill to own.

FIND A WALL: Back yourself up against it, see how you'll surprise yourself. Lean into anxiety.

CHAPTER EIGHTEEN

Set Your Own Course To Win

Taking Control of YOU

Who is your most important client? That's easy, it's you. Never lose focus on yourself or your direction.

It takes a pretty strong mindset to chart a course focused on becoming a better, bigger, and bolder you.

When you consider that a more impressive you can do a lot of good for others and put some time and effort into setting your schedule with purposeful meaning, good things happen. When you figure out how to use your greatest strengths and gifts to deliver for others, things begin to change.

I remember the first time I created that logo for Kann Advisory Group, and I just sat there at my desk and stared at it. I also remember the first shipment of clothing that came to my house – my company name, big and bold, embroidered, and ready for the outside world. Opening the box filled with shirts and sweaters and pullovers with my brand on it was a bit of an eye-opener. And kind of scary.

Putting yourself out there for the world to see takes a mixture of guts and confidence. But the thing I kept telling myself was that I wouldn't be doing it if I didn't think I had something worthy to share with others.

Think about your career journey and the various stops as an investment.

Investing in your 401k is important for your future retirement and a comfortable life after years of hard work. Investing in yourself along the way is what allows you to extend the life of your career and build the legacy that will forever be attached to your name.

Here are some things to remember and questions to ask that are tied to building your brand.

- **What will you do or say that is special and unique?**

  When you put your own personal plan into motion, make sure your message is authentic and fresh. Your spin on something and being able to deliver it well is what makes other people take notice.
- **What will people think about you?**

  We live in a world where people are quick to judge first and *then* think about it later. We will never get around that. Letting go of stress about what people will say is the first key to delivering something that gains traction and has long term sustainability. There will always be people who will question you internally. Just keep delivering things that move the ball forward.
- **What will people say to others about you as a person?**

  Many people feed off critiquing others. That won't change. Perhaps it's their way of deflecting the disappointment they feel about themselves onto others. Work to do work that rallies people for the common good. If it's a presentation, make it inspiring. If it's a project, put something together that gives people reason to tell others about it. You control your own narrative. Remember that. Do positive things and you will get positive feedback.
- **What will people tell others about what you say?**

  This is my favorite question. What you say has powerful impact. What we say creates a feeling from others about how they view us. What we say directly impacts what others will say. That's what I want. I want word of mouth marketing and you should, too. Next time you have an audience, think carefully about the message you are delivering and, most importantly, think about what others will say about the message itself. Build your comments around how you think you'd like others to react.

Here are a few examples:

The special teacher is the teacher who delivers more than the daily curriculum. Be the one who adds something special that students will remember years later and talk about at their reunion.

The special financial analyst isn't the one who puts a spreadsheet in front of the client with the numbers they expect to deliver based on buying and selling and maneuvering of your monetary assets. Be the one who connects with the client's children as well. When they're in high school, first learning the importance of spending and saving, give them an early start that will last them a lifetime.

The special presenter is the one who does far more than just stand before the group going through visual slides and sharing information. Be the speaker who spends time before and after the talk connecting with audience members. Be the speaker who doesn't just give a talk, but instead delivers an engaging experience that leaves everyone talking *about* the presentation.

If you want to be relevant in your business or industry, then make sure you focus energy on doing something unique and relevant.

The quest for relevance in our world requires us to jump outside of the norm and do things or be someone who stands out. Only when we focus our time and energy on things that *are* relevant – to our mission and to others – will we truly become relevant.

Being relevant results in being requested.

People are attracted to people who bring something to the conversation that is worth remembering. We remember those who share something special or who do something others don't or won't think of attempting.

I've been in many meetings focused on taking care of the client. At the end of the day, building a company success story means starting with *you*. After all, a commitment to becoming a more attractive and magnetic *you* is what landed the client in the first place. Right?

If you want to win with your story, start committing more time and more energy on becoming the best brand you can be. Take control of you first, make yourself valuable and interesting to others, and others will follow your impressive lead.

KRAIG'S LIST

3 THINGS: Your Track to Relevance

SELF AWARENESS: Know who you are and want to be. Be your own best client.

PURPOSEFUL WORK: Being relevant means time spent doing relevant things.

A PATH NOT TAKEN: Don't follow the curve. Find a way to set one that's worth following.

CHAPTER NINETEEN
Become An Influencer To Win

Paving Their Way Helps YOU

The most significant impact you can make is to add personal and professional value to others. If that isn't the true measure of success, then what is?

Here I am, writing a book about the importance of storytelling and brand building as a way to elevate your personal and professional platform. And there is one word - above all - that I believe we should all strive to have linked to our name.

The word is "influence."

I am a firm believer that influence grows with effective communication, sharpened messaging, dynamic presentation skills, command of media opportunities, and unique value associated with your social media sites.

In my *"Elevate Workshop,"* I talk a lot about influence being:

- the capacity to have an effect on the character, development or behavior of someone or something
- a person who sways opinion or is able to make an impact

In my mind, influence means you have some important traits that allow you to make a big impact on people. Anyone looking to create a powerful brand for themselves probably has at least a few of those traits.

Among them, I believe valued knowledge and experience in a given field are critical to influencing others. Having and owning an opinion is also big, as is the ability to deliver it in your own way and with a style that is yours, and only yours. Also key, is consistently sharing information that adds real value to others. In other words, is there a positive connection that comes from the information you share? Can people relate to what you are sharing and is it something worth sharing with others?

KRAIG'S LIST

3 THINGS: Influencer Status Requires

KNOWLEDGE: Experience in your field above others.

ORIGINALITY: Opinion, delivery and style unique to your field.

VALUE CONTENT: From voice to print, make your message count for something.

KANN LEADERSHIP

Here now is a select group of people who've uniquely shaped my personal story. Each meant or did something special for me. Each is someone who's been the subject of stories I've shared with others because of the impact they've made on my career and my life.

Included are professional mentors who have reached great heights in their career or field of choice. Others are family members, or coaches, or people I've looked up to and tried to emulate. Or, maybe, someone who's helped me through a tough time and helped me re-focus or see a new path when navigating anything at all seemed tough.

Each influencer is uniquely mine. My "influencer."

William Harvey – My Grandfather

For me, it begins with my late grandfather, Bill Harvey.

My mom's father, Bill Harvey, was there for me as a child and really never left. As a child in Chicago, my grandparents lived just a few blocks from my house. That made weekend visits very convenient. He was there on Saturday mornings to play games. I would go to his house for sleepovers when my parents were out for the night and sometimes even when they weren't. He and my grandmother, Margaret, were a huge influence on me.

"Gramps," as I called him, was the "injured man" when I played the role of surgeon as a kid. He was the guy who got off work early to come watch my weekday middle school basketball games. He was the guy who took me out for my first round of golf. He took me on in ping pong, and to this day, I believe he let me beat him.

When he retired and my grandparents moved from Chicago to Peachtree City, Georgia, he and my grandmother drove up to Chicago to grab my brother and me and drive all the way back. Sure, I flew sometimes. But this gave us extra time in the car, meals together and hotel nights and memories I've never forgotten.

My grandfather was "the fun guy." He was also strong and firm when he needed to be. When I started my television career, he told me that I'd need to outwork people and find a way to be different. He also told me never to badmouth people because it would be more of a reflection on me than on them—a great lesson.

When I reached the Golf Channel, he made sure to upgrade his cable service to make sure it was on his plan. And he would call me to comment on the show and call my mom to talk about the outfit I was wearing. He was proud and he made sure I knew it.

I learned a lot from him; how to be a father beyond just what I learned from my own dad and also how to work hard and have fun. Our years of playing card games and watching sports and playing golf taught me that work isn't everything and his words of wisdom during those moments together never left me.

He made sure my own kids knew of him. He was there for them too, as a memorable great grandfather.

I made sure to visit my grandfather before he passed. And if there is one story that says it all, it's the vision I have of him being in Orlando with my family a few years after my grandmother passed away.

He had made the journey from Texas to Orlando to spend time with us and that included one of my son Trent's travel baseball games. His presence wasn't much different than what he had done back when I was a kid, except for one thing.

My son hit a home run that day for his great grandfather to see in person. I'll never forget it. Neither has my son. Life is about being present. And when you *are* there, make sure you are *all* there. Bill Harvey always was.

Ken Kann – My Dad

Ken Kann was an only child. Like me, he grew up in suburban Chicago, and he, too, attended a pretty sizeable high school. He was a three-sport athlete at Oak Park River Forest, and my guess is the Huskies were better off athletically and academically because of him.

My dad spent the lion's share of his professional career at Harris Trust & Savings Bank in downtown Chicago. He took the commuter train back and forth every day. My dad was a man of habit. And as I recall, he had the train schedule memorized down to the very minute and he took the same train down and the same train home. As a youngster, I could walk out to my sidewalk just after six o'clock at night and see him coming down the street on the three-block walk from the train station in our hometown of Western Springs.

Because he was so established in his routine, we never ate as a family until after seven when he was ready. As I got older, that wasn't a big deal because I never got home from practice until after six. But as a kid, waiting until after seven was tough. And there was no budging him.

My dad would disagree with this, probably, but he had a drinking issue.

Every night after returning home, he would have his martini and then a few beers along the way before he turned in for the night. What I saw was something that stuck with me for years. I never saw my dad drunk, but we all knew that he had an issue. And it was mood altering for all of us.

Ultimately, it affected his relationship with my mom, and they divorced late in my college career. I saw it coming. I wasn't surprised. I don't say all this to clear the air or lay blame. I don't think there really is any harboring ill will. Certainly not from me.

All that said, my dad was a really good man. And he loved me. And he loved his family. I knew it and I never once questioned it. Like my grandfather, my dad attended every sporting event I took part in that he could possibly make. He left work early for high school baseball games and never missed one of my football Saturdays that I can remember.

Dad gave me the love for sports that became my career. Every night he came home, I stole his sports page that he'd read on the train and I covered it from front to back.

He helped me with my homework and was brilliant at math and was great when it came to English papers. He was a freak on grammar and as much as it drove me crazy, he taught me the importance of speaking clearly and properly.

Perhaps most important, my dad shared one thing with me that became my push.

He spent nearly forty years of his career in the same industry and at one banking institution. He traveled quite a bit for many years, including some international travel. But he never pushed me into his line of work. Instead, he said, "follow your own dream." He told me to chart my own course and never wavered from it.

No one was more excited about my decision to attend the University of Missouri for its renowned journalism and broadcast program, and no one was more excited about my journey toward whatever was to become my first big job destination than my dad.

In television, that became the Golf Channel. Dad made some trips with me, including a fun day in Chicago for a shoot that led to him meeting major champions, Lee Trevino, Craig Stadler, and others. He loved every part of that day.

Religiously, Dad took me to Butler National Golf Club in Chicago as a child each year for the PGA TOUR's Western Open. That was his way of introducing me to the game. We sat on the hill and watched guys like Jack Nicklaus and Tom Watson – even Mark Lye, who would become one of my closest friends in the golf television business.

Years later, while working for Golf Channel, I tried to take him with me to *The Masters*, but he was not feeling well and said he just couldn't make it. I'd never get the chance to ask him again.

While in Hawaii for a tournament a few years later, he shared that he had been diagnosed with colon cancer. That was January of 2002. I was devastated. I spent the next five months traveling between tournaments and a hospital in Chicago. Dad lost his battle and passed away on May 15, 2002. He was just sixty-eight. He died far too young.

I'm left with a lot of memories and some sadness that he never really met my youngest daughter, Kendall, who was born in November of 2000. While he spent time with my twins, he passed when they were just five and never saw them play baseball, football, volleyball, or cheer at the big games. He'd have been proud. I'd bet a lot of money he'd have moved to Florida to make sure he saw them in action.

Maybe you can relate to this. Like all of us, he had his shortcomings, but seeing it and living it made me a far better father along the way. Above all, his influence was about dedicated hard work and his consistent support for my dreams. And it stands out to this day. He encouraged me to carve my own niche and find a way to make a difference.

Shouldn't we all.

Dick Wojick – My High School Football Coach

Having played many sports as a kid, I've been blessed to have some great coaches along the way.

And then there was Dick Wojick. Forty-two years as a head football coach in multiple states, he won seventy-six percent of his games and is a member of the Illinois High School Coaches Hall of Fame. He was my varsity football coach at Lyons Township in LaGrange, Illinois, and the dad of my best friend Dave Wojick, who was our quarterback.

Long before he was my coach, he was the head of the household at the house I spent a lot of time visiting. His greatest influence came a few years before I was a member of one of his most talented teams – the 1983 Lions he coached to into the state playoffs.

Back in 1980, I was a freshman. And before the first game we played, I injured my shoulder at practice. A dislocation or subluxation as it's termed, which is pretty painful. I felt the need to quit, which I did. Much of the reason was that I didn't want to ruin my chances of playing basketball.

He pulled me aside at his house and gave me some tough love and counsel. He was firm on the idea of not throwing away my years of football over one injury and a belief that, in his mind, I had a future in the program that he didn't want to see me toss aside.

After rethinking things, I rejoined the team, rehabbed my shoulder for what would be the first of many times, and went on to have a nice high school career. I've never forgotten that talk.

Upon my request for this book, here's what Dick shared to me about the idea of "influence."

"The success of coaching young men is not measured in the number of victories, but in the number of young men who go on to be good people, good parents, good workers, good leaders, and good role models for others. Sports serve as the building block of character in which you build your life around. It's not so much about where you are when competing but where you are headed and where you will end up.

Sports parallels life and in winning and losing, we should be taught to be humble in both. In winning, we need to use victory to climb to the top of the mountain. And in losing, we need to find lessons and work to make sure it never happens again.

Individual successes lead to team successes and we are only as good as those we surround ourselves with. In life, we must never forget the importance of listening and learning as we will always have to answer to someone and need the ability to accept criticism and learn from it, while also receiving praise and using that as a catalyst for growth."

I've been so fortunate for coaching in life. Among the things he taught me was that the minute we stop allowing ourselves to be coached, we are missing valuable lessons we can learn from and share with others.

Kent Collins - University of Missouri School of Journalism

Aren't we all influenced by teachers? Isn't the role of a teacher one of the most important things in each of our lives?

Like you, I'm sure, I've had some great ones. Many served as mentors and I could list a handful that gave me tools that have served me incredibly well along the way. But one college professor stands out.

Kent Collins is a hall of fame member in the Missouri School of Journalism. He has molded many into becoming successful journalists around the world. In Kent, those who set foot on campus with a broadcast journalism dream had a front-row seat to someone who made it his mission to inspire and instruct. In that order.

"You can't preach to anyone unless you can get them into the church," said Kent whenever he had the audience.

I've never forgotten it. And I can't be alone.

In writing this book, there was no way Kent Collins would be left out. Here's what he offered up on the topic of "influence" and his opportunity to influence others in his role as one of the leading broadcast journalism professors in the country.

> *"In our current culture, being an influencer means promoting a product or service or idea that people buy. And the influencer makes money. But for a teacher or college professor, being an influencer has a longer shelf-life than 'point of purchase.' Teachers and professors influence for the long term.*
>
> *For me, influencing results in two key payouts. First is seeing former students become good journalists at television newsrooms around the country, around the world. In some small way, my influence helped make a newscast anchor in Chicago or win an investigative journalism award or create a new and reliable news organization. That's a commercial payout. But second is seeing former students provide their communities and country with information that they use to exercise our American democracy. That's the great payout of being an influencer.*
>
> *As an influencer, I am long term. My brand is to continue to influence people in their first jobs, their ongoing careers, and – most importantly – in*

their application of journalism skills to the important issues that Thomas Jefferson said are vital to American democracy."

Kent's influence carries well beyond me and my journey. I'd bet thousands could tell a similar story of his impact. We were all fortunate.

Michael Whelan – Former Television VP & Executive Producer

His call went to my agent. That call then circled around to me while working as a sports anchor in Kalamazoo, Michigan. Michael Whelan was an Emmy and Peabody award-winning executive producer for HBO and NBC Sports before he was named Vice President and Executive Producer at The Golf Channel.

His brand is one of creative genius with a confidence that he could build a network programming line-up from scratch. That's exactly what he did at Golf Channel. Scratched out on a napkin, his vision of studios, shows, and talent on both sides of the camera came to life in a short period from 1994 to 1995.

Over the years, Mike has been a different person to different people. To me, he will always be the maestro of bringing the vision held by Golf Channel founders Joe Gibbs and Arnold Palmer to life under the bright lights.

He gave me the opportunity to interview for what would become my "big break."

Years later, his influence is still there with me. And he shared these thoughts about the topic of influence and brand.

Today, the term "influencer" is somewhat broad and describes anyone who causes a reaction in others, or, impacts the way others feel. Whether it be to follow this person or tune in here, an influencer has incredible power. When you boil it down, an influencer can effectively point people at a specific concept. This power comes in many forms, including authority, specific knowledge, industry relationships, or one's corporate position.

My mother taught me how to be a good human being, which ended up translating into a great, well-respected boss. A well-respected individual will always be an incredible influencer.

At the time of my hiring in 1994, The Golf Channel was only a concept. I was able to turn it into a reality, and my job was to create the entire look of the network. A great influencer cannot be afraid. Once a person becomes afraid, they stop communicating, and that destroys any hope to be a successful influencer.

A brand is built on respect. I had the creative and management responsibility of painting a network that the home viewer would forever mark on their calendar as "must-see TV!" I became a world-wide influencer based solely on the consistent quality television shows I produced, directed, and wrote.

Molly Fletcher – Agent, Speaker, Author, Entrepreneur

The further you advance in television or media, the more important it is to have someone who can sit across from executive decision-makers and negotiate your contracts. But an agent is more than that and Molly Fletcher was far more than that for me.

She was CSE's top media agent for several years, negotiating deals on the agency's behalf for names like broadcasters like Ernie Johnson and Clark Kellogg, coaches like Tom Izzo and baseball stars like John Smoltz.

Molly just has "a certain way about her" is the best thing I can say. She put me in the right mindset during great times and some challenging moments as well.

But it's not what Molly did in that role that influenced me as much as what she launched for herself when she made her own career pivot.

Post agent career, Molly has become a renowned leadership and career coach. The Molly Fletcher Company has taken off much because of her ability to connect with people and push them toward a better self. Her "game-changer" approach and podcast are inspiring and her ability to succeed as entrepreneur, author and speaker gave me the belief that I could do the same.

Here's what Molly shared about the power of influence.

To know that my words can change someone's life, move them through a challenge, and allow them to lean into needed change is humbling. As a former sports agent for almost twenty years, athletes have a short window of time to do something very few have the chance to do, often on a world stage. As a speaker, I again have a short window of time to make an impact on an audience's life. Influence, be it as an agent or speaker isn't motivation or management, it is unlocking in others their best self, being their guide. I am grateful when people come up to me after a keynote, our workshops, or the emails and letters people share when they say, "you hit me" " I get it" sometimes I see them smiling and sometimes their eyes are filling up with tears, but either way I know my words connected, inspired and influenced them to believe they have more to give.

My platform as my client's agent was to maximize what is often a short window of time and influence it in ways no one else could. To have the courage to have tough conversations. To have the trust to tell them the truth and have them know it was coming from a place of love. And most of all, to remain consistent and help hold them accountable to their dreams. Now, as a speaker and author, words, energy, and insight become my platform to inspire and change not just athletes but leaders and emerging leaders. I share one of a kind of stories from my days as a sports agent who brings to life the behaviors of the best athletes and coaches in the world. The goal is simple; connect these stories back to the audience in a way that shows them a process and path toward their best self. As a wife and mother coming from a male-dominated world, I'm grateful for a platform that invites connection to both men and women, young and old.

I've seen Molly speak. Ironically, we found ourselves on the same speaker schedule a few years back at a marketing summit for SAP - a major corporate organization. I made sure not to miss her message that day.

I am so grateful for her honesty in managing my television career during the time we spent together. But I'm even more appreciative of the conversations we've shared about making the most of every stage and finding a new avenue of success sharing years of experience with audiences looking for a message they can use in their daily life.

She's a difference-maker of the highest order.

Arnold Palmer - World Golf Hall of Fame, Co-Founder of Golf Channel

In life, each of us comes across someone who just stops you in your tracks and makes you think about everything you say and how you carry yourself around them. With every meeting, be it one or multiple, you are left to wonder that they thought and what they'll remember about you. Arnold Palmer was a legend in golf, an icon in sports, and a superstar person.

Palmer didn't officially hire me at Golf Channel. But his commitment to building the network allowed others to make that decision. And I am forever grateful. I loved the place. His place.

The late Arnold Palmer is so much more than major golf championships and bringing golf to television in a way never before seen. He was everybody's friend, whether you knew him or not.

He was someone my grandfather and my father admired. Millions would have given a lot just for one meeting or a quick photo. I was blessed for more than that.

So how did he influence me?

He did it the same way he did it to everyone he came across. He did it with class. He had a smile every time he greeted you. When he walked through the building at the Golf Channel, he made people feel important and was grateful to see and connect with stewards of his investment and ambassadors of the game he helped shape.

Any picture you had taken with Arnold Palmer became a prized keepsake. And if you ever spent time with him on the range at Bay Hill Club and Lodge in Orlando, you just knew it was his home club. You could feel it because he made you feel welcome. He made me and everyone feel *at home*.

As my years in golf carried on, "The King," as he will always be referred to by everyone, gave me inspiration to give back to the game in a positive way. When it comes to delivering talks or working with specific groups in golf, I try to give them a little something extra because of what golf has meant to me. That's what Arnold Palmer always did.

Sadly, Arnold Palmer passed away in 2016. We are all left with memories. I especially like this quote, attributed to him.

> *"Golf is deceptively simple and endlessly complicated; it satisfies the soul and frustrates the intellect. It is at the same time rewarding and maddening – and it is without a doubt, the greatest game mankind has ever invented."*

Because of Arnold Palmer, I now always try to look people in the face with a smile and create the same warm connection. And I've shared that with my children as they grew into young adults.

In short, Arnold Palmer is everything that positive "influence" stands for. I wouldn't be where I am today if not for his effort to create "golf's channel."

David Swanson – Lead Pastor, First Presbyterian Church of Orlando

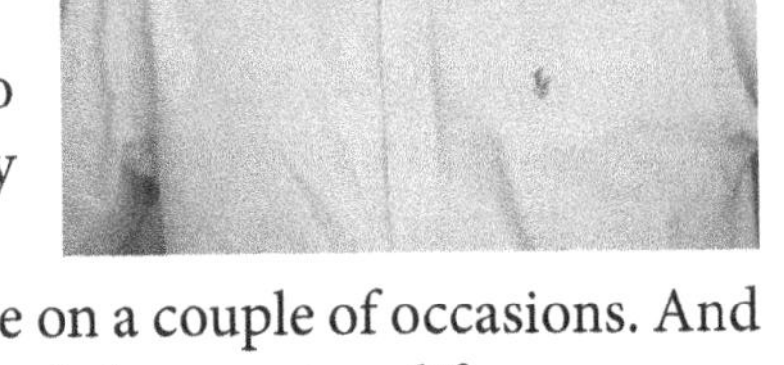

I've been a churchgoer since childhood. Yes, my parents made me go to church.

In Chicago, I was a youth group member through my four years of high school. Somehow, I was actually chosen to give the sermon to the entire church on Youth Sunday one year.

As an adult, I became an advocate of church and its many benefits for my own children.

Sometimes in life, things seem to go along so well that we don't think we need church to carry on.

Then divorce hit me. My career changed course on a couple of occasions. And through it all, I admit that, at times, I felt lost. I needed a re-set on life.

Even as a confident person, I needed a boost.

That came in the name of David Swanson. The pastor of one of Orlando's largest congregations, I was blown away by his message one Christmas Eve and made it my mission to meet with him and make his church my new regular place of worship. I went alone. We've become friends ever since.

People say that God only gives you what you can handle. I used to believe that. Now I disagree.

David helped me understand that God gives you moments where you feel like you can't handle anything on your own so that you'll turn to him, and others.

I asked David for his words about "brand" and the platform to influence others. Here's what he says.

> *Being an influencer as a pastor has been one of the great joys of my life because it has filled me with a daily sense of meaning and purpose. Every day, people are trying to navigate their way along this journey of life, and I am traveling with them. My perspective is slightly different. My position on the road is not quite the same, but we are figuring it out together. As we do, I have the privilege of infusing the journey with the presence of God. I am trying to help people see the world through His lens, not theirs, and that one visual change can make all the difference. I am also privileged to be with people in their most painful and most joyous moments, moments in which I try to point to the generous and merciful Hand of God.*
>
> *My platform puts me in a place to help people see the world differently and to learn about the things of God. Thus, I am not trying to build my brand, but His. I am the moon; Christ is the sun. Whatever people see of God in me is only reflected glory. I am not the source; God is, and so my task is to humbly share my own broken nature, God's redeeming work, and the hope He gives to all. If the life we seek is found in the true life of Christ, then yes, I believe that is the brand to follow.*

The best influencers are able to create a bigger following.

Growing your followers gives you a wider reach and a bigger audience to share your message. David is a dynamic speaker with as much passion for preaching as you will see live and in person. David has a following. And David has a follower in me. Because of him, I'm also a believer that tough times lead us to a better place, the right people, and a chance to see who we really are.

Because of his influence, I now have a message stronger than just my expertise in communication, branding, and media. I have a story people can relate to. And that is the most important thing you can have when connecting with your audience.

Hailey Kann, Trent Kann & Kendall Kann – My Three Kids

Any parent who says their children don't influence them isn't telling the truth.

As much as we share our experience and knowledge with them, they also share things with us that help us become better ourselves. Aside from the memories, we have with them, to me, that's the very best gift we can get from our children.

I once heard that when it comes to parenting, we have to remember that we aren't raising children – we are raising future adults. That's so true. And it's powerful.

Hailey and Trent are twins and four years older than my other daughter Kendall. All three found their way to the University of Missouri, just as their parents did. Amazing how that works. Many have chuckled about that. And, yes, there was some influence at play there as well.

Each of them brings unique strengths to the family and each has provided a loveable challenge or two along the way.

Together, and separately, I have been wowed by how they have handled their successes and failures. I've also greatly appreciated how they've handled mine.

Seeing their ups and downs and negotiating their emotional challenges, they have coached me more than they would ever know. They have taught me to prioritize whenever possible. They have taught me the need to truly *be there.* And *they*, while not knowing it, have also pushed me to work harder and more strategically so that I could give them - and also me - more time for what is important in life.

Lastly, and most importantly, they have shown me the need to be me and build me.

In growing older, they've found their own way of doing things and created an independent path toward their own future, which leaves a parent like me left alone in a way to find a life separate from the daily routine of raising and living with kids. It's not easy. Not at all. The empty nest can be a place of unforeseen quiet that causes a lot of internal noise about where life has gone and where it will go.

What now? What next? How will I fill my time? What's my new purpose?

They've pushed me to focus new energy on my life and my legacy. Years from now, what will they say to each other about my influence? What will they do for themselves because of what I've done and how I have lived? What will they share with others about me and my purpose and my parenting?

As parents, we often talk about the gift that comes from *being a parent*, right? Well, how about the gift they give us and the influence *they* have on how we carry ourselves?

Think about it.

I know I've been pushed to better on every television or radio show, in every speaking engagement and in every staff meeting and every leadership workshop because of the experiences and responsibilities given to me by my children.

They, while not knowing it, played a huge part in me writing this book. I have always been motivated by my role as a dad and giving them the best of me at every opportunity. I hoped that in writing this book, I give them some better insight into me and my own story.

A few years ago, I told them that birthdays and holidays would no longer be as much about me giving them gifts. Instead, I would focus more on creating time and memories.

I hope this book becomes a keepsake for them. I also hope it—in writing instead of the usual in-person "Dad lecture"—shows them the gift of what is possible for each of them. I hope it tells them that their story is important too. And, that someday, their years of experience will be worthy of someone else's attention.

Our kids are our greatest blessing. Over the years, I think every parent hopes to influence their lives in meaningful ways.

But in saying that, I'm pretty confident we can all look back on the many ways we've lived out *their* influence.

Who are ***your*** influencers?

Who are the people who've left their mark on you? Who taught you things you've never forgotten and things you've used throughout your journey?

If you could sit back at the end of your road and say "thanks" to a few people who've given you motivation, delivered opportunity, or shaped you in a way that has made you, you; who would they be?

Make your own list, and you'll quickly see the value they've added to your story and the way you'll tell it.

If you want to win with your story, understand that a brand is built over time, and much of who we are is because of the time we've spent with our most special people. Put those people in your story.

KRAIG'S LIST

3 THINGS: Great Books That Influenced Me

LINCHPIN - Are You Indispensable?
Seth Godin

THE START-UP OF YOU
Reid Hoffman and Ben Casnocha

PLATFORM - Get Noticed in a Noisy World
Michael Hyatt

KANN LEADERSHIP

MY STORY

What's Next

Why I Want To Go There

Writing this book has forced me to take stock of my career and also my life. It's amazing what happens when you begin to put it on paper and how it stares right back at you. I'm glad I've done it.

I'm proud of my run to this point. If I've learned one thing about myself over the years, it's that I struggle to stand still. I think status quo causes one to become stale. At least for me it does. Businesses that succeed never sit still and neither do the leaders who run them. They're always adapting, always changing. If they don't, if we don't, we quickly get passed by.

I am having a blast standing on stages, in front of people in conference rooms, and now in front of computer cameras, presenting my story and helping others to effectively do the same. I'm enjoying the look in people's eyes as they go through my leadership communication workshop. And I take great pride in my consulting business that helps people and organizations discover exactly who they are, uncover the best of themselves, learn their story and be able to present it as they've never done before.

If You're Smiling, They're Smiling Too

I thrive on the opportunity to share and mix it up on the radio and other media platforms. I love hosting my podcast.

From here? Who knows for sure. Who really ever does?

I rule nothing out. But I do have one rule for my future. I don't want a "job" per se. I want the next great opportunity to allow for the chance to showcase what I do and specifically, how I do it. It's all about the chance to make a difference for others. If that means building Kann Advisory Group as my long-term commitment, then that's great. I love doing what I do and I will push to make it better.

But if something unexpectedly presents itself, and I can take my media and communications experience and combine it with my entrepreneurial background to become a great fit for a corporation or business tied to sports, I'm wide open to that as well. Maybe I can do both. Actually, that screams being a consultant.

Limiting myself isn't in the cards and I wouldn't recommend it for you either - especially with what I've seen and lived.

I was talking recently with a woman I greatly respect for her ability to identify talent and give them the stage to represent one of the biggest brands in the world.

Her name is Meg Green.

A talent recruiter for ESPN, she has spent the last couple decades seeking out rising stars and people who bring unique presentation skills to a roster of on-air talent that now includes more than eight hundred.

Meg and I met years ago while I was at Golf Channel and happened to be covering the PGA TOUR's tournament in Hartford, which is just a stone's throw from ESPN's headquarters in Bristol, Connecticut. We met in a hotel lobby that week as opposed to her office so as not to start rumors of me seeking a new job. I learned a long time ago that word travels quickly and I needed to protect myself from a false storyline. My agent team at CSE had set me up to meet Meg and the conversation was not centered around the possibility of a job, but instead just a chance for me to hear what people in her role truly look for while also giving us a chance to get acquainted.

My fear was always that I would get labeled a "golf guy" and so I was always looking for ways to spread my knowledge and grow my network.

What I took from Meg then, and have discussed with her over the years since, was the need to continue to "evolve."

That's an important word.

In one conversation, she talked to me about how she and her team identify special talent within her organization that might just be "the next big thing." In deciding whether they can handle the biggest stage, the network provides "stretch opportunities" in the form of shows, bigger games to be a part of, or live situations that they haven't yet tackled. It's not just a one-shot deal they're given, but perhaps a week in a given role or a series of shows to see how the talent evolves and improves. Conquer the moment, she said, and upward mobility is sure to follow.

How does that apply to us?

It is my opinion that while we might not exactly know what our "next" might be, we should always add new skills to our tool box, new people to our rolodex and perhaps venture into new things that add to our profile. Each new thing becomes our opportunity to "stretch."

This book has been a "stretch opportunity" of the highest order for me. A blog was a big challenge before that. And the podcast – *TRACKS TO SUCCESS: Inspiring People & Inspiring Stories* - is my newest "thing." We'll see how far I can take it.

Kraig's Podcast – Sharing Success Stories

As I move forward, I don't want to give the same keynotes. Paid speaking is a rush just like television and radio to a degree. I want it to expand and I want my platform to become bigger and I'll aim to deliver my keynotes even better. I want my workshops to include new twists and give greater value to new and bigger clients. I would like the "group" in Kann Advisory Group to become a bigger more noteworthy roster of expert talent who add greater value to what I am able to share. And I'd also like to share it more internationally and not just in the United States.

We are all subject to change. Working for an organization or any boss means we are moments away from structural change that could leave us looking for our "next."

And I can't emphasize strongly enough that we need to develop ourselves and expand our talents and skills every day, every month and every year so we are ready for the "next" before we're forced to find it.

A few years ago, I found my way back into broadcast media after a call came my way to join SiriusXM as a host on the PGA TOUR channel.

Kraig on SiriusXM – A Childhood Dream Realized

After about six years away, I was thrilled about the opportunity to be back in the game of golf and do something different. I had never done meaningful talk radio and it was something new. It challenged me and it has given me the media voice I put on hold when I left Golf Channel and became the LPGA's Chief Communications Officer.

Did I see it coming? No. Am I glad it came? Absolutely. Radio is something that's had my interest for years. As a guest on many shows during my career, I was always intrigued to host a show myself. I just figured I was a "TV guy" and radio might not be in the cards. Now, it's something I hope will carry on for a long while. I consider myself fortunate.

But a role on radio won't define me. Just as television didn't and just as every other role hasn't. I think I'm at my happiest when I'm reaching many audiences and doing multiple things. At the same time, I have enjoyed the chance to be my own boss and find new platforms to grow my own brand.

Finding one's voice and building your story is a process. But like everything, it requires patience. It evolves over time. I'm excited about what's ahead and where the path might take me. Just remember, before you can effectively tell your story, you have to truly live it. The details are yours to own. It's probably swirling in your head somewhere. The fun will come when the moment hits you.

CHAPTER TWENTY
Always Say Thanks To Win

This Book Doesn't Happen Without YOU

What we do and what we achieve shouldn't define us. How we get there doesn't happen alone. A successful brand means doing something that benefits others and remembering those who've made a difference in your climb.

Sit down sometime and make a list of the people who have helped you. Finding our voice and broadcasting our story isn't a solo act. Not even close. It takes a loyal foundation of people committed to your path – past and present – and your ultimate goals and dreams.

I owe a thank you to my Mom and Dad, who bought me the first tape recorder and microphone that I used in my room to broadcast my own games. And I owe a thank you to my friends who came over and sat beside me as my fellow "commentators."

I owe a thank you to my seventh and eighth-grade basketball coaches, Joe Obucina and Gary Wagner, who gave me the confidence that helped me – not just on the court, but off it.

I owe a thank you to Pastor David Hedlin, my high school youth minister in suburban Chicago. He made church meaningful for me long before I sat in churches listening intently to Pastor Bill Barnes or Pastor David Swanson in Orlando.

I owe a thank you to all the talented people in my broadcast journalism graduating class at the University of Missouri. It showed me just how much I would have to put into my chosen field to land a job and make an impact.

I owe a thank you to my tight circle of best friends who've been with me during my toughest personal times and supported my career choices and the many challenges along the way. Guys not previously mentioned like Ted Cox, Bill Waliewski, and Jerry Magee.

I owe a thank you to every boss I've ever had for their counsel, positive and negative, and the chance they gave me to learn and grow and try to make an impact.

I owe a thank you to established and respected news anchors like Jim McLaughlin in Ft. Myers, who showed me a level of professionalism in television that served me well for years beyond my time working with him.

I owe a thank you to every producer or director and all the studio production folks in my television career who made me look better than I probably deserved. Two who made me clearly better were Matt Hegarty and Kevin Schultz from Golf Channel.

I owe a thank you to every media member who helped me in my role at the LPGA to elevate the level of awareness the organization deserved. And to every LPGA player who took a seat on my player communications committee. Beyond being star players, they were star people.

I owe a thank you to Kent Skornia, a trusted business advisor, author, and leader of a major St. Louis financial company who once hired me to speak at a Mizzou athletics golf fundraiser. Bigger than that, his professional guidance has provided results for me and my business that I couldn't have attained on my own.

I owe a thank you to Mike Waddell. A former college athletics director, we met in 2009 on the sideline at a Cincinnati-South Florida prime time football game. He's been a loyal friend ever since, helping me grow my media coaching business and giving me the microphone as the public address announcer for the Orlando Apollos of the now-defunct Alliance of American Football, where he was the team's president. That was a blast.

I owe a thank you to Jon Newsome, the CEO of Presentation Partners, who's believed in me from the day I ventured out as a speaker. His company has invested in me, designing my slides and creative content that has truly brought all of my speeches and presentations to life.

There are so many more, But I owe my greatest thank you at this point to my kids; Hailey, Trent and Kendall. Earlier, I mentioned them among my greatest influencers. Simply stated, the older I get, the more I value the life I've had with them.

Long gone are those days when I'd show up on the screen, they'd hear my voice or see my face and say, "hey, there's Daddy on the TV!!" As time advanced for them, it became just another television or radio show, podcast or speaking engagement. Nothing special. And that's just fine. In their eyes, the light on Dad might be a bit dimmer as the spotlight turns more in their direction. That's how it's supposed to work. But, through every one of my pivots, transitions, good times or bad, I've always felt that they've respected my career and my choices. And since they're not slowing down, I figure I'd better keep up a good pace and keep striving to do more and do it better!

I've met so many people and have had so many amazing relationships in my career. But there's no single target audience more worthy of long-term personal investment than your family and your children.

The higher you climb, the better you should treat others. If it's the opposite, their influence will halt your progress or leave you empty when you reach the top.

After each presentation I give, I'm always grateful for the line of people, no matter how long or short, who have taken the time to come and chat. Their "thank you" is not only flattering, but also serves as a huge motivator to stay on track. My track.

After all, without a supportive audience, what do we really have?

No matter how many people are in front of you, the goal should be the same. Give people a message worth remembering and an experience worth sharing with others.

We make a name for ourselves one relationship at a time.

One handshake.

One smile.

One loyal supporter.

This book is the combination of a belief I had that I could put my words together into something that others might find compelling and something with value. In other words, I believed that I had some things worth sharing.

It is also the result of many people giving me enough positive validation that some of the things I've said or done have lifted them up and provided them with messages and information that had really helped them in their career and life.

In short, there is a pretty decent chance that you – yes, you – have played a part in me putting this together. Maybe you watched me on television or heard me on the radio. Or maybe you saw something on one of my social media platforms. Quite possibly, you have attended one of my speaking engagements or workshops.

All I can say is thank you. And it's probably not enough.

For you, my advice is that when it comes to speaking to a group or something as small as a staff meeting or conference call, make sure to let people know you appreciated them hearing your presentation.

I have made it a point to spend time before and after my presentations with the people who have written the check to bring me there. My best practice is to come in the day before and offer to join the executive team or any collection of leaders on hand for dinner or a drink and a small bite. This serves as an ice-breaker for all of us and a chance to spend some quality time off the stage with key people in the organization.

If that isn't in the cards, I will make sure to spend the same amount of time meeting people and delivering small conversations before and after my talk. In other words, if I'm asked to speak for an hour, I'll make sure to stay for an hour after the talk if there is free time to spend, rather than rush back to my hotel room or the airport. I don't like to feel like I'm "in and out" with no care to deliver beyond the talk that's been asked of me.

Our brand depends on the feelings of our followers. And the more time we can spend talking and connecting with people – free of asking for something – the better impression we can make. Sometimes we don't get much time. I'd suggest making the most of what you get.

We all have a network of followers and supporters. If you want to win with your story, it's your job, in our most unique way, to take good care of them.

KRAIG'S LIST

3 THINGS: Critical To Your Success

A NETWORK: People who know your worth and won't stray are like found gold.

AN AUDIENCE: People in front of you give you the gift of opportunity... to influence.

A FOLLOWING: People to thank. They've seen your value and are emotionally moved to support.

KANN LEADERSHIP

MY STORY

I'll Leave You With This

Three for the Road

You can work to be comfortable, or you can work to be outstanding for you and others. It's your choice to make.

No matter the business you're in, no matter the goals you have, always remember that you are the chief marketing officer of yourself. It's your own brand and your brand to own.

From day one at Golf Channel, each of us was tasked with properly representing the rest of the people in the building and the stakeholders who trusted the channel as a place to invest their time and money. I took enormous pride in the brand itself, and when I held a microphone or sat on the studio set wearing one, I made sure my own brand represented the network and its people in the best way I knew possible.

Every day I went to work at the LPGA, I was trying to create new opportunities for the players on the tour and the membership outside the ropes. As a collective group of leaders, staff members, players, or teachers, we aimed to showcase the tour itself in a way that raised its profile and showed it well.

And that thought process is something that I think we should all work toward. Every day, we should go to work with a purpose - and a plan. Otherwise, what's really the point?

I read recently that great leaders are motivated by the answers to two questions:

- What keeps them awake at night?
- What makes them get up in the morning?

Representing the LPGA at the White House

As I have told groups, "what we do means a lot, but how we do what we do means a whole lot more." I'd say that trying to put that thought into play probably answers the above two questions for me.

Here are five things I've learned and experienced about the process of one's career:

- **Having a goal isn't just some thing, it's the only thing**—I knew from the time I was about seven years old, I wanted to be a television sports commentator. As you now know, I did high school games on radio, I went to the University of Missouri solely because of its highly respected journalism program. I did sports television internships to prepare for jobs after college. And I worked my way through local markets to the Golf Channel, where I was a host for seventeen years. I had a goal to get there. I didn't know where "there" actually was. But I stayed focused on my goal and my dream. To me, we are nothing valuable without ambition.

- **Goals begin to change, it's a given**—As my Golf Channel career progressed, I began to take an interest in the business side of sports and found passion and energy in the idea of sharing ideas to create a better product. Ultimately, it led me to start a business of my own, which I parlayed into the great fortune that became the LPGA opportunity. Overseeing communications for five years gave me more than I could have imagined, allowing me to spread my wings and grow.
- **Priorities change too, count on it**—When you're young and fresh out of school, you'll do anything and for however long. You are focused on climbing the ladder at all costs. As your career winds, the ideas of family and time become more important. Don't get me wrong, career goals and passion remain, but not without internal conflicts and competition for time. I'd say that it's ok to yield as needed. It makes you better when you *are* working.
- **Connect and network, yesterday**—I've had wonderful opportunities to speak to students at various universities. The one that stands out is Mississippi State and its PGA Golf Management students. Standing in front of nearly 100 students in an auditorium, I made it clear to each student that the friend sitting next to them is also quite possibly their biggest competitor for a job. As well, the person seated next to them on the other side might actually hire them someday. It works like that. Jobs are precious and so are relationships - so build them and help others before you need them. Don't collect business cards, gain value from people, and tell them how you can help their cause before thinking about what they can do for you.
- **Branch out and brand yourself**—What are you known for? Everyone is known for something, but is there only one thing? I was proud to be an ambassador and host for the Golf Channel. Hearing, "Hey, it's the Golf Channel guy," was flattering. But I wanted to grow and I wanted to learn new things and add value to other causes. That mindset still motivates me. Starting my first media consulting brand - HTK Media - in 2010, hosting college football and basketball for XOS Digital/SEC Digital Network, speaking to students, corporations, and business groups was the launching pad for what ultimately became Kann Advisory Group.

My guess is you've experienced some of the things I have. My advice is this: don't shy away from the stress of internal questions and some conflict within yourself. You might benefit from thinking outside your own box. When it comes to stress and anxiety attached to your career, lean into it.

In my workshops and speaking engagements, I leave people with three final thoughts. I call it "*Three for the Road*" and so, here we go. These are questions only you can answer for yourself.

Sharing Insight with Titleist Sales Leaders

First, *Are you better or different?*

Please find confidence in yourself and remember that your story matters. Nobody knows it better than you. Act on that as soon as possible. Find a way to sharpen your edge and separate yourself from the pack. More importantly, find a way to do what you do differently. That's how people take notice.

Second, *Are you saying something that means something?*

How many times have you been in the audience listening to somebody speak and when they finish, you don't have a whole lot to say to anyone else about the experience? Be the person who leaves a mark. Remember, the size of the room isn't what matters. It's the people in it and how you make them feel. Give them a real message. Don't just speak at them, connect *with* them.

Third, *Are you ready to stand out?*

Don't wait to figure out who you are, what you stand for, or how you'll present yourself from here forward. Understand that a focus on building your brand doesn't mean you're self-centered or wrecked with ego. Your job is to leave a legacy. Your job is to make a difference. You can't do it by standing still. You have to stand out.

I was on a phone call once with an industry connection who had watched me on Golf Channel and tracked my career beyond. He made it a point to tell me he was happy for all my success.

Obviously, I was thankful for his comment.

But what does "success" really mean? His definition is probably different from yours and, most likely, different from what I'm thinking. I hung up the phone, stopping the task I was about to return to – which was to finish writing this book.

I thought for a few minutes about what he had said and my mind went back to something I have said to others. Maybe you buy into it and maybe you don't.

To me, success isn't about money or career advancement. It's about what I've written below.

The biggest impact you can make is to add value to others. If that doesn't define success, then I don't know what really does.

My challenge to you is to put more focus on what you are doing to impact others and more time on how you are creating opportunities for yourself to do more of it. When we make the most of every opportunity that comes our way, more seem to follow. That is called positive momentum.

Author and motivational speaker Jay Danzie took the business world by storm with this globally recognized quote:

"Your smile is your logo; your personality is your business card, how you leave others feeling after having an experience with you becomes your trademark."

For each of us, there are so many platforms and so many ways to make a difference. Believe it or not, people are waiting for you to stand up and then stand out. So why not start now? Design your own experience to share with others and create your own trademark.

It all begins with you and the time you'll put into yourself.

Figure out who you are and why people should pay attention.
Broadcast your story.
Build your following.
Grow your brand.

In no time, you'll have found your real voice. You'll have become a communicator who gets other people talking. And as a result, I think you'll be impressed with everything that comes your way.

Building Brands with Corporate Leaders at Diamond Resorts

KRAIG'S LIST

3 THINGS: Big Topics
Big Questions

YOUR BRAND: Are you ready to be better ... and different? Build your legacy.

YOUR COMMUNICATION: Are you ready to say something that means something? Build your message.

YOUR STORY: Are you ready to STAND OUT? Build your following.

KANN
LEADERSHIP

POSTSCRIPT

A Pool Of Ideas

I love the idea of creating ideas. The true challenge is making the most from the pretty good ones.

It's pretty amazing what twenty minutes in the pool swimming laps can do for your mind.

Believe it or not, the real concept for how to present this book came from the calm waters of the gym I belong to in Orlando, Florida. I'm at my best when I'm dedicating myself to a regular fitness routine. I'll never say I'm the most physically fit guy, but I can definitely speak to the fact that when the gym is a regular part of my routine, I'm at my mental best.

Working out gives me clarity on what I need to do and what is or isn't really important. For some reason, I seem to work problems out in my head a lot better in goggles and a swimsuit than when I'm at a desk or driving in a car talking on the phone.

I don't know where your best thinking takes place. But I do know that thinking is some of our best work. If we have no distraction, we can focus. When we focus, everything becomes possible. When I'm in the pool, or on a treadmill, my mind goes in so many directions about the job that I have and the places it can take me and the people I can meet and the possibilities that can come from all of that. As I have said already, the only problem is that, for me, idea overload is an issue from time to time and I'm challenged to sort out the good from the bad.

I was once told that if you have ten ideas, you actually have none. I agree. Too many ideas create confusion and anxiety. With that, I do my very best to narrow the focus and rally myself around a simple few that I'm willing to commit to seeing through.

As I swam laps one day, the entire concept of this book fell into place.

Finding your voice. Broadcasting your story. Building your brand.

We all strive to be heard. We all want people to listen to us. We all hope that what we say has value to those on the receiving end. In other words, we want to talk and we want people to be impacted by what we have to say. It's really that simple.

The problem is that many of us aren't all that good at delivering our message. We can all be better.

From the time I was a young kid, I was always talking. Yes, that's the truth. I never had a shortage of words and was always pretty good about finding an audience that would give me a shot to present my latest story. My career would ultimately be all about talking. And it still is.

It bears repeating that, for me, the key to effective speaking is that you have something to say. Nobody wants to just listen to people talk.

So, I'll toss this on you before we're done. Based on everything I've shared in this book, please give yourself some extra credit and learn the value in your own story and learn how to share it. Consider yourself just like a corporation seeking loyal customers and a big piece of the market share. Realize that you do have a brand.

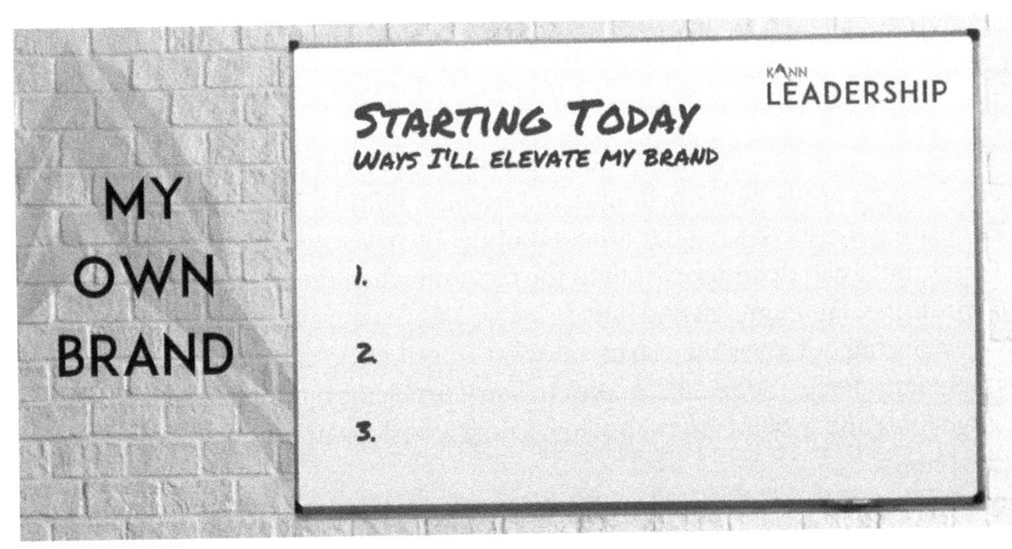

And it was bigger to start with than you had ever given it credit for. Now, work hard on building it and work even harder on the ways you can share it with others.

And remember, have no fear. Put it all together and push forward with confidence in your ability to get our attention and make a real difference. You'll be surprised where it can lead you.

EPILOGUE
What If

What if, the place where you had devoted the majority of your professional career suddenly made good on rumors and officially told you and the rest of your co-workers that the company headquarters was relocating? And what if, in the same announcement, employees like you were told that jobs would be terminated.

Remember my earlier chapter titled "What Else Ya Got?"

In June of 2020, The Golf Channel announced that at year's end the main facility in Orlando would be closed permanently and most of its operations would be moved to Stamford, Connecticut which is home to NBC Sports Group. Employees were put on notice that they would would be without work unless offered a position that transferred.

Remember my comment about building yourself a "second something?"

Waves of job cuts at Golf Channel began at the end of August and were to continue through the end of the year. As I took in the news from my own home office, I saw the wave of social media posts as well. Many who I had worked with and many I didn't know began reaching out, changing profiles on LinkedIn and requesting to connect.

Remember my topic of preparing yourself for a next act in your career?

The Golf Channel has been a huge part of my career. I'm hardly alone. I feel for those displaced and left searching for a new home to call "work." COVID, the global pandemic that cut to the very core of the American economy in 2020, didn't have anything to do with what was really a business move to keep costs in line with profits. Much is sure to change with regard to programming and much has already changed in the lives of many.

The Golf Channel is hardly the only company forced to alter course. Employees who built its

Golf Channel's Launch Night – January 1995

foundation, laid its cable and broadcast its signal are certainly not the first to go through a traumatic and seismic career shift.

COVID forever changed the narrative of world history. Loss of job can forever change a person's career narrative as well.

The question then becomes; would you be prepared for a sudden job search?

Hopefully, you've taken stock of your own career path, goals, passions, talents and offerings well before a career emergency might possibly land on your doorstep.

This is where all that I've discussed about years of strategically building a network of people that can guide and counsel you as much or more than they can hire you comes into play. This is where being a valued expert in your field and not just a contributor gives you a leg up on competition. This is where years of building a brand before you truly need it makes a difference.

As I discussed, for years I felt labeled as a golf-only broadcaster simply because I was loyal to a job I loved. Unfortunately, nearly two decades calling or talking about golf doesn't translate very well into a smooth transition calling college football or basketball games or sitting in the studio breaking down the Chicago Bulls, Bears or White Sox – no matter how much I know about those teams or their sports.

So, my final thoughts are that you think about the title of this book and the importance of getting people to see you and your resume for something unique and different. Find your way to delivering noteworthy value in your industry well before you are put on the clock to land your "next."

Put yourself out there. Do it now. Do a temperature check on how the industry values you before you're at the doctor dealing with anxiety and panic.

Build your tool box of talents so you don't have to hammer on so many doors. A brand that's been worth following for years leads to doors opening on their own and a belief that you have something special to offer – even in times when jobs are scarce. Be the person companies can't believe are sitting on the sideline. You can

With Chris McCallum, Titleist

With Katherine Rentner, SCI Lighting

With Bill Bowman, Falls Lake Insurance

create future leverage with current effort by building a story worth sharing and one that people remember.

In my workshops, I preach about being the person in the room who stands out. I put value on the person who can get our attention by presenting themselves more uniquely than others. That person is awarded "the green shoe." Green because it stands out. Green because it gets people's attention. As much as anything, it's a reminder of the mindset that blending in doesn't cut through all the noise.

Remember my point that we can't wait for other people to take notice of us and do the work of putting our name, talents and brand forward. We have to put our energy into doing things worth paying attention to and make them take notice.

What if, you're the person who gets their attention? What if you're the person with the best story to tell? What if you're the person who stands out among the rest?

Time to put in the work to make it happen. Time to become a brand new you.

Good luck!

Acknowledgments

Books don't just happen. They're born from inspiration and a will to create. I owe thanks to some very special people who deserve credit for this book that is now in your hands.

My dad passed away in May 2002. I wish I could thank him in person. Ken Kann was my everyday supporter, a motivator and someone who always pushed me to reach for things that gave me a sense of pride and accomplishment. This book qualifies. Cancer took him from us too early. I miss him every day. And if I was signing book copies before they hit the shelves, he would get the first one.

To say my Mom has been a supporter would be the strongest of understatements. If you know Joanne, you've experienced her loving, caring way. She has always been my proudest promoter. For that, she will deservingly get my first signed copy. Thank you for being the Mom who has always been there with a desire to give and for listening as much as you have always found ways to show love.

Thank you to my amazing kids; Hailey, Trent, and Kendall. Born in that order, I put you equally on my highest pedestal. You are loved more than you will ever know and with the opportunity to be your parent, you have provided me with life's greatest gift and shown me a father's most important purpose. I am honored to be your Dad and forever blessed because of our memories together. I hope this book shows you the importance of working in your own way to positively impact others.

If you are my true friend, I trust you know it. As you read this book, I hope you relived a few stories and experiences. They shaped me in so many ways for the better and I want you to know that our friendship inspires me to find the good in others and be that same friend as well.

Lastly, I owe a great deal of gratitude to Vinny D'Assaro at CSE for helping me pursue this venture. And also, to Cathy Teets and Headline Books. Together, you enthusiastically believed in my story and embraced my vision to deliver something people would pick up, purchase, and be proud to promote as something well worth their valuable money, time, and attention.

To you, the reader, thank you so much for investing in me and my written words. I hope you'll enjoy this book which is my way of investing in you.

Photo Credits – Thank You To:
Golf Channel, LPGA, WWMT-TV, Missouri Lottery,
North Florida PGA, Duncan Littlefield, Gabriel Roux